GUIDE TO
ANCIENT BRITAIN

D1014229

GUIDE TO ANCIENT BRITAIN

BY

BILL ANDERTON

foulsham

LONDON • NEW YORK • TORONTO • SYDNEY

foulsham

Yeovil Road, Slough, Berkshire SL1 4JH

ISBN 0–572–01620-4

© 1991 W. Foulsham & Co. Ltd.

Acknowledgement is given for photographs to Bill Anderton, Paul Devereux, Mick Sharp and the Welsh Tourist Board.

Printed in Great Britain at St Edmunds Press, Bury St Edmunds

For Eileen

'Occult' means secret, or hidden, and suggests discoveries to be made that are beyond ordinary human experience.

CONTENTS

HOW TO USE THIS BOOK

This *Guide to Ancient Britain* has been written and designed for explorers, travellers and tourists, interested in visiting ancient sacred sites. First, you can choose easily the type of site that you would like to visit in a particular locality. Then the short descriptions will provide the sort of information that makes the particular feature come alive for you, as well as providing basic information about use, size, age and so forth.

This will give you a way in to making your own deeper explorations and discoveries.

So that you can plan a route which takes in perhaps several sites in one trip, the entries have first been organised into geographical areas. Then within each area you will find a map showing where the sites are in relation to each other, and on which page they are described. The order of the entries in the book has been chosen to make travelling easy from one site to the next. You will find an alphabetical index of all the sites mentioned at the back of the book.

Having decided where to go, you should consult a road map, as the 'how to get there' descriptions will guide you, by road, to the locality of the site that you wish to visit. Many of these features require more accurate directions to find them, and so a specific Ordnance Survey map reference is given at the top of each entry. Some general road maps use this system, but a large-scale Ordnance map will always prove to be worthwhile.

Under the heading 'Food and Drink', I have chosen a town near to each particular site and provided the address and telephone number of one or two recommended hostelries. You may well find what you need closer to the site you are visiting, depending on your needs, but the entries included may nevertheless prove helpful. I recommend that you telephone to check on the type of services provided.

So, it couldn't be easier. This travelling companion will tell you what you can see, how to get there, what it's all about – and then after this sustenance for the soul, you will find it for the body too! Happy hunting.

Bill Anderton

INTRODUCING THE SACRED SITES OF GREAT BRITAIN

I do not claim to be an expert in earth mysteries, archaeology, ancient history or the like. But I do profess to an interest, even a compelling fascination for the mysterious, and for those places in our landscape that inspire awe and a sense of the sacred.

I know that I share this with many other people, and it is to them that this book is directed. To visit an ancient sacred site and soak up the atmosphere created by history is to experience something that can never be conveyed in words. It is what Paul Devereux in his superb book, *Earth Memory*, calls 'Being and Seeing'. You have to be there to appreciate the real meaning and significance of any verbal description.

The basic facts cannot convey this experience, but what they can do is lay the foundation for simple enjoyment or perhaps a deeper experience. It is possible by 'being and seeing' to obtain insight into the purpose of an ancient site or to experience what have been described as earth energies.

Compiling this book has been a thoroughly enjoyable experience. It has been a great pleasure to visit as many of the sites that I describe as possible, and to collate information about them, drawing on the expertise of others more knowledgeable than myself. To these expert researchers and their insights I owe a great debt.

Wherever you may be in Great Britain, you can be sure that there is a site nearby worth visiting and exploring. There are hundreds, so this book provides only an indication of the possible pleasures and experiences to be had. There are many, many places not included for the simple reason of available space, and the research time that was available to me. However, you will find a carefully selected cross-section, with longer descriptions of the more important sites such as Avebury, Stonehenge and Callanish.

The sites chosen are not based simply on their attraction as prehistoric centres. Many places containing occult dimensions may have begun life before the dawn of history but their power to evoke the sense of something great in the universe, and in ourselves, has echoed down through the years – the sites have been used continually and sometimes converted from their pagan beginnings into Christian usage.

When Christianity came to these isles, one secret of its success was in the way it adapted local sacred sites for its own ends. In the same way, much older festivals of the year were taken over and adapted in some way.

Hence, a church may have been built on a site used for, perhaps, religious purposes well before Joseph of Arimathea arrived on these shores bearing the sweat and blood – and the message – of the Christian saviour.

You will find herein many examples of occult symbolism existing inside sanctified ground, so your explorations will not necessarily take you to the bleak outposts of Dartmoor or the Outer Hebrides.

The message of ancient times, rites, customs and the ancient sense of oneness with the earth and the universe is written all around us. This guide is designed to help you to unravel these secrets and see them for yourself.

When visiting these places, please do so with a sense of respect, both for those who will come after you and for those who over perhaps thousands of years have been there before. It is only if you know how to be and see at a sacred site or centre that its occult (literally 'hidden') aspects will be revealed to you.

The process of collecting information, sifting it, visiting and selecting sites for inclusion in a guide such as this is a never-ending one and I hope to edit a sequel in due course. If therefore you can let me know of any special places of occult interest that you think I might like to know about, please write to me c/o the publishers, W. Foulsham & Co.

Finally, I refer readers to the article on dowsing or 'divining', appended to this book (see page 210). This is by Dr Arthur Bailey, a good friend of mine, who successfully practises and writes about dowsing and its various applications. Dowsing is becoming ever more popular as a way of delving into the unknown, whether the search for answers be directed under the ground, or into the minds of the builders of an occult or sacred site. You might like to try it and see if it works for you.

SCOTLAND

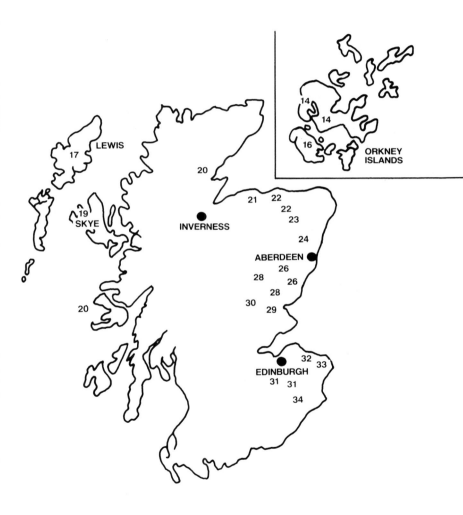

RING OF BROGAR

Stone circle – symbols

Orkney   MAP REF. HY3213

The Ring of Brogar is an outstanding stone circle, found on Orkney's mainland. It measures approximately 105 metres in diameter and 27 of the original 60 stones still stand, though others are still close to their original locations. The tallest of those standing is 5 metres high. The placings of the stones, done with extraordinary precision, suggest the use of the circle as a lunar observatory. One of the broken stones is inscribed with ancient, undeciphered tree runes, indicating some magical use. There are numerous surrounding standing stones and connected smaller circles: a treasurehouse for the researcher into earth mysteries.

Clearly signposted on the A965, the circle is between the lochs of Stenness and Harray.

Food and Drink: In Kirkwall at Ayre, Ayre Road (0856 3001).

MAES HOWE TOMB

Burial mound – power point

Orkney   MAP REF. HY3213

Near Stromness, on the island of Orkney can be found the remains of a magnificent chambered tomb. The

1. Ring of Brogar

tomb lies beneath a 7-metre-high mound of clay and stones, the entrance being through an 11-metre-long passage lined with huge slabs of stone. The chamber of the tomb measures 4½ metres square. The wall opposite the entrance and the two side walls each have a recess leading into the body of the earthen mound. Burials may have been placed within these recesses. The tomb was sealed in about 1500 BC, and remained thus until AD 1150 when it was broken into by some Norse pirates who were spending the winter on the island. Nothing was left in the tomb except for some runic inscriptions testifying to their presence.

These inscriptions were carved by Vikings over 800 years ago, but the beautifully constructed cairn is dated to about 2750 BC. It is orientated so that the midwinter sun shines down the 11-metre-long entrance passage to light up the inner beehive chamber. Among the carvings on one of the uprights is the famous Maes Howe Dragon.

15

East of Stromness on the A965 route to Kirkwall, the tomb is close to the Loch of Harray. Maes Howe is signposted near Tormiston Far, about 5 km on the A965 west of Finstown.

Food and Drink: In Stromness at Hamnavoe Restaurant, Graham Place (0856 850606).

RACKWICK TOMBS

Earthwork – power point

Orkney   MAP REF. HY2400

One of the two rock-cut tombs in the British Isles is found below Ward Hill on the island of Hoy. The chamber has been cut by hand and measures about two metres in length. It is of excellent workmanship and could have been used as a chamber for initiation ceremonies. The blue sandstone into which the passage is cut is today called the Dwarfie Stone. The other rock-cut tomb is to be found in Glendalough, Ireland.

Hoy can be approached by way of Stromness, on the mainland. The stone is a few hundred metres to the south of Rackwick Road, below Ward Hill.

Food and Drink: In Stromness at Hamnavoe Restaurant, Graham Place (0856 850606).

2. Rackwick Tombs

CALLANISH

Stone circle – standing stones – power point – rituals

Isle of Lewis   MAP REF. NB2133

The pilgrimage to this most remarkable of stone circles is an experience never to be forgotten. The location of Callanish to the west of the Isle of Lewis is one of splendid isolation, the complexity of the ground plan an inspiring discovery. The ground plan reveals the complex to be a sort of crossed circle, with a northwest avenue approaching the central circle of 13 stones, varying in height up to 3.65 metres. There are several other less impressive circles in the vicinity, all seemingly related to cosmological calculations and effects.

Within the Callanish circle is a chambered cairn dating back to around 2000 BC, close by the entrance to which stands the tallest monolith at over 4.5 metres. The whole complex was probably the ruins of a combined temple and community centre.

Every 18½ years, at a time known as a major standstill of the moon, this orb will rise just above the horizon, which it then skims, rising no higher, then to disappear from view at its setting. The parallels of the stone avenue point to the set of the moon at the southern extremes of a major standstill. When the circle is viewed from the north, the moon sets at this time into the midst of the stone circle, leaving a series of gleams and 'after-glow' effects among the stones. The long axis of the Callanish circle is directed to the point of moonrise, while a number of stones within the circle are orientated during the time of skimming to several other outriders to fix the point of moonset.

Callanish is signposted off the A858, west of Stornoway on the Isle of Lewis.

Food and Drink: In Stornoway at Seaforth, James Street (0851 2740).

3. Callanish, looking SE at the central circle enclosing a monolith and a small passage grave

4. Callanish, looking down the main avenue

DUNVEGAN CASTLE

Legend – fairies – symbols

Isle of Skye, Highlands   MAP REF. NG2549

The Fairy Flag is a silk banner which hangs in Dunvegan Castle. It is reputed to have been given to the fourth Lady MacLeod in the fourteenth century by a woman in a green petticoat who was a fairy. The 'flag' was said to have given the MacLeods the power to cope successfully with three crises: in 1490 at the battle of Glendale, in 1580 at the battle of Waternish, and the third . . . is still to come. Although somewhat tattered now, the so-called 'elfen spots' of crimson can still be made out.

Dunvegan is on the A863, north-west of Glamaig on the Isle of Skye. The castle is signposted on the A850, about 2 km to the north of the town.

Food and Drink: In Dunvegan at the Dunvegan (047022 202); or Harlosh, Dunvegan (047022 367).

FINGAL'S CAVE

Power point – legend

Inner Hebrides   MAP REF. NM3335

Fingal's Cave although a creation of nature holds a mystical atmosphere surpassing the mysterious attractions of the greatest man-made occult centres. When the poet John Keats visited it in 1818, he wrote to his brother to say that in 'solemnity and grandeur it far surpasses the finest cathedrals,' and the old stories of the giant-builders came easily to his mind.

Fingal's Cave is on the island of Staffa, most easily reached from the island of Iona. Landings are not guaranteed as the weather is notoriously changeable.

Food and Drink: In Tobermory, Island of Mull, at Ulva House (0688 2044).

DORNOCH

Church – symbols

Highlands   MAP REF. NH7989

Look for the exterior gargoyles on the cathedral of Dornoch, said to be the oldest church in Sutherland, although most of its stonework is modern reconstruction, with a little surviving work from 1224. Look also for the Green Man nature spirit on the front of the west porch. This pagan image has been Christianised by having the tendrils weave the form of a cross over his head.

Dornoch is at the eastern end of the A9(T), on the spur of the A949. The cathedral is in the centre of the town.

Food and Drink: In Dornoch at Dornoch Castle, Castle Street (0862 810216).

FORRES

Witchcraft

Grampian   MAP REF. NJ0358

The metal plaque by a witch-stone, set in the retaining wall of the A96, states, 'From Cluny Hill witches were rolled in stout barrels through which spikes were driven. Where the barrels stopped, they were burned . . .' There were once several witch-stones in Forres, but this is one of only two that remain today.

Forres is on the A96(T). The witch-stone is on the south side of the road, almost opposite the police station.

Food and Drink: In Forres at Ramnee, Victoria Road (0309 72410); or the Royal, Tytler Street (0309 72617).

BURGHEAD HOLY WELL

Holy well – paganism

Grampian   MAP REF. NJ1169

Sometimes called Bailey's Well or the Roman Well, this ancient work was discovered in 1809 and assumed to be of Roman origin. The well is a rock-hewn chamber to which steps have been cut. A platform leading into the waters suggests that it may have been used by the early Christians for baptisms. However, artefacts, such as images of the pagan bull, have been found on this site, demonstrating that it was used by the Picts, if not actually built by them.

Burghead lies at the end of the B9013, signposted north of the A96(T), west of Elgin. The well is in a continuation of King Street, off Church Street.

Food and Drink: In Elgin at Laichmoray Hotel, Station Road (0343 540045); or Mansion House, The Haugh (0343 48811).

ELGIN MUSEUM

Symbols – ritual

Grampian   MAP REF. NJ2162

The most interesting exhibit, for those involved with esoteric symbolism, to be found at the Elgin museum, is the Burghead bull. This is a Pictish stone carving found during the excavation of the well at Burghead.

The museum is founded and funded by the Moray Society.

Elgin is on the A96(T), to the east of Forres. The museum is centrally located.

Food and Drink: In Elgin at Laichmoray Hotel, Station Road (0343 540045); St Leonards, Duff Avenue (0343 7350).

LOANHEAD STONE CIRCLE

Stone circle – power point – witchcraft

Grampian   MAP REF. NJ7528

Standing in the parish of Daviot is the Loanhead Stone Circle, which is a recumbent cairn circle, flanked by a smaller circle. The historian Dalyell records that about ten people were burned to death at 'Loanhead' in one single execution for the crime of witchcraft.

Daviot is signposted to the east of the B9001, north of Inverurie. The circles are signposted, and are approached through woodlands.

Food and Drink: In Inverurie at the Gordon Arms, The Square (0467 20314).

5. *The recumbent stone at Loanhead*

SUNHONEY STONE CIRCLE

Stone circle – engravings – ritual

Grampian   MAP REF. NJ7407

There are several recumbent circles found in this part of Scotland, and one of the eleven standing stones here is touched by the recumbent flat stone, itself about 6 metres long, towards the southern end. The stone is said to be directed towards minimum full midsummer moon, and it is deduced that the circle must have been part of a larger calendrical system. There are 28 cup marks on the recumbent and these may have been used in establishing points of orientation.

About 2 km north of Echt, on the B977, to the right-hand side, is Sunhoney Farm. The circle is above the farm, up an unpaved cart-track, in a distinctive circle of trees. The circle lies on private land, so obtain permission from the farm to view it.

Food and Drink: In Banchory at the Burnett Arms (03302 4944).

6. Sunhoney recumbent stone circle looking NW at cup marks on slumped recumbent

ST VIGEANS

Stone carvings – occult symbols

Tayside   MAP REF. NO6342

Beautifully displayed in a tiny museum there is a fine collection of ninth-century Pictish stones, bearing some of the symbols which, for all their Christian intentions, must be called occult. The guide states, 'They demonstrate no artistic or cultural antecedents.' The Drosten Stone is a two-metre slab, incised with a cross, a serpent, a dragon and a hunting scene, along with an untranslated inscription.

St Vigeans is north-west of Arbroath, signposted off the A933. The museum is part of the terrace of houses opposite the hill-raised church.

Food and Drink: In Arbroath at Hotel Seaforth, Dundee Road (0241 72232).

ABERLEMNO STONES

Standing stones

Tayside   MAP REF. NO5255

Three impressive Pictish stones stand along the road in the village of Aberlemno, with carved occult symbols suggesting three different styles in their employment. The Aberlemno stone stands in the church graveyard. This is another eighth-century Pictish

7. *Churchyard cross, Aberlemno*

stone, adorned with what appear to be hunting or battle scenes. The face sports an interlace cross with flanking dragons and grotesque beasts.

The roadside stones are on the eastern side of the B9134 in Aberlemno. The church is to the east of this road.

Food and Drink: In Brechin at Northern, Clerk Street (03562 2156).

GLAMIS MANSE

Standing stone – stone carvings – power point

Tayside   MAP REF. NO3947

A Pictish stone bearing carved symbols stands nearly 3 metres high. The elaborate decorations include an intricate cross, surrounded by the figures of men and animals, and symbols. This type of carved stone is only found in north and east Scotland. The designs most frequently seen include animals, birds, snakes, fishes, objects such as mirrors, combs and swords, and geometrical shapes. It has been suggested that the stones were intended as tombstones and the earliest ones are thought to pre-date Christian influence. Later slabs depict Christian symbols, and by the end of the tenth century, the older symbols had died out.

Take the A94 west from Forfar to Coupar Angus and Glamis is at the junction of this road with the A928.

Food and Drink: In Glamis at Strathmore Arms (030784 248).

DRONLEY

Legend – symbols – monument

Tayside   MAP REF. NO3437

The carving on the St Martin Stone is Pictish in origin

and shows a man on horseback spearing a snake-like dragon. This large stone marks the spot where a mediaeval damsel-devouring dragon was killed by a man called Martin. Local names, such as nearby Strathmartine and the village of Boldragon, signify connections with this mythological deed.

Dronley is signposted off the A923. The St Martin Stone is signposted from Dronley.

Food and Drink: In Dundee at Queen's, 160 Nethergate (0382 22515).

SCOTLANDWELL

Holy well – power point

Central   MAP REF. NO1801

It is said to be at this holy well that Robert Bruce was cured of leprosy, and records show that Charles II travelled from his Dunfermline Palace to take the waters, while Mary Queen of Scots too visited the well. An inscription above the water fount gives the date 1858, but this refers to the reconstruction. This well, like all Scottish holy places, is very ancient. The waters from the fount can be drunk from a special metal cup which hangs nearby.

The well is signposted to the right of the A911, to the west of Kinross.

Food and Drink: In Kinross at Kirklands Hotel, High Street (0577 63313).

DUNNING FOUNTAIN

Magic – alchemy – symbols – memorial

Tayside   MAP REF. NO0114

The fountain in the village square of Dunning is decorated with symbols on its four faces, each relating to the four elements of Fire, Air, Earth and Water. Each elemental symbol is, however, related to water: the Fire element is represented by a newt, the Air element by a water-fowl, the Earth element is a frog, while the Water element itself is represented by the image of a fish in the mouth of a seal. In astrological lore, the Fire element is characterised by energy, activity and creativity, Air by communication and the intellect, Earth by the physical body and matter, and Water by the emotions.

To the west of the village is a dramatic memorial to witchcraft. It is a cross raised on a mound of local stone on which is daubed 'Maggie Wall burnt here 1657 as a Witch.'

Dunning is at the junction of the B8062 and B9141, south-west of Perth. The memorial is on the road to Milhaugh.

Food and Drink: In Perth at Salutation, South Street (0738 22166); or Timothy's, St John Street (0738 26641).

ROSSLYN

Church – hermeticism – numerology – symbols

Lothian   MAP REF. NT2663

At the church of St Matthew at Rosslyn, the Rosslyn Chapel is still privately owned by the Earls of Rosslyn. Of special interest to occultists is the series of pentagrammic stars fashioned in the main roof, proclaiming a numerological significance, and which recall a similar use of stars inside certain of the inner chambers of the Egyptian pyramids. There is also a collection of grotesqueries and demons inside and outside the church. Look for a pair of striking gargoyles above the north doorway and a splendid horned demon is to the left of the interior window immediately to the right behind this door.

Rosslyn Chapel is in Roslin, signposted to the west of the A6094, south of Edinburgh.

Food and Drink: In Roslin, at the Olde Original Rosslyne Inn, Main Street (031 440 2384).

TEMPLE

Occult centre – temple

Lothian   MAP REF. NT3158

The Knights Templar were once active in this hillside village whose ruined thirteenth-century church is a testimony to the ancient link with this mystical order. The church was partly rebuilt after the order was suppressed in 1309. For those interested in occult symbols, the gravestones and memorials in the burial grounds are well worth exploring.

Temple is signposted to the west of the A7(T), south of Edinburgh. The ruins of the old kirk are towards the bottom of the village, to the left.

Food and Drink: In Howgate at Old Howgate Inn, Ester Howgate (0968 74244).

SPOTT

Power point – holy well – ritual – witchcraft

Lothian   MAP REF. NT6775

An annual procession made by the Knights Templar, said to have been held on St John's Day, passed through the churchyard and church, which then had a different orientation, before descending to a holy well, used as a focal point for the processional. The mediaeval roof above the well is in reasonable condition, although the well itself is now dry.

Spott Loan is a road near the village which was used in the seventeenth and eighteenth centuries as a place for burning those condemned for witchcraft. A witch-stone, set back from the road, marks the place of one such burning.

Spott is signposted off the A1, south of Dunbar. The

well is approached by a pathway to the west of the churchyard.

Food and Drink: In Dunbar at Bayswell Hotel, Bayswell Park (0368 62225); or Redheugh, Bayswell Park (0368 62793).

AUCHENCROW

Witchcraft – legend – rituals

Borders   MAP REF. NT8561

Look for the witch-stones in this village. One is built into a retaining wall at the western end of the village street, while another, hidden behind brambles and nettles is nearer to the centre of the village. Charles Walker's researches in *Occult Britain* reveal that this latter stone was called the Peg Tode stone. When passing the stone, children were required to say, 'I touch Peg Tode, Peg Tode don't touch me.'

Auchencrow is signposted off the A1(T), south of St Abbs Head.

Food and Drink: In Berwick-upon-Tweed at Turret House, Etal Road, Tweedmouth (0289 307344); or the Queens Head, Sandgate (0289 307852).

EILDON HILLS

Power point – legend

Borders   MAP REF. NT5432

A man walking on these haunted and magical hills came across the underground cavern where Arthur and his knights slept, awaiting their call in the time of England's need. He also found a sword and a horn hanging from the roof. He blew the horn and was swept from the cavern by a magical wind. On telling his story to some shepherds, the man died within seconds, without revealing the location of the entrance to the cavern.

The Eildon Hills lie to the south-east of Melrose.

Food and Drink: In Melrose at Burt's, Market Square (089682 2285); or George and Abbotsford (089682 2308).

8. Eildon Hills

NORTH

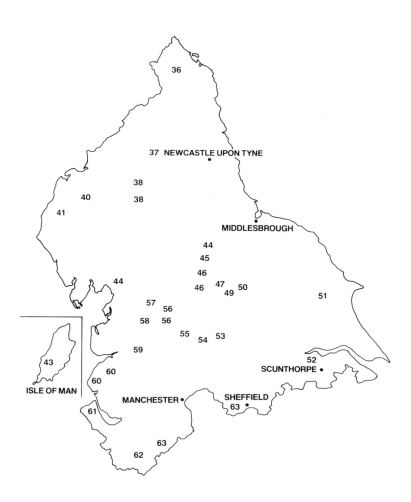

36

37 NEWCASTLE UPON TYNE

38

40   38

41

MIDDLESBROUGH

44

45

46

44   46   47   50
                      49

57   51
   56
58   56

55   54   53

59

52
SCUNTHORPE •

43
60
60

ISLE OF MAN

MANCHESTER •   SHEFFIELD
                      63 •

61

63

62

OLD BEWICK

Stone carvings – symbols

Northumberland   MAP REF. NU0822

The ancient engravings on this stone show clearly the carved cups and concentric rings and channels which go by the name of 'cup and ring' marks. Several theories have been put forward to explain them although their origin and purpose remain obscure. They are found mainly on rocks in the north of England, in Scotland and in Ireland. One theory links them with mazes, while another describes how they were maps, revealing the locations of other ancient sites in the area. John Foster Forbes believed that, 'There is an affinity between these cups and the nature of the stars. A star is a generator and transmitter of Cosmic Energy in spiral form. These cups could be used as micro-cosmic examples of spiral-staral energies.'

Go north on the B6346 Alnwick to Woolar route before it joins the A697.

Food and Drink: In Powburn at Breamish House (066578 266).

CARRAWBURGH

Temple – power point – symbols

Northumberland   MAP REF. NY8671

The remains of a Temple of Mithras built in about AD 205 are to be found among the ruins of what the Romans called Brocolitia, to the south of Hadrian's wall. The present layout is an archaeological reconstruction of the temple's destruction in about AD 297. Some of the pagan Mithraic symbols have survived into modern symbolism, most notably the zodiacal Taurean bull. Mithras, a Persian sun god, popular among the Roman armies, brought with him an esoteric lore and symbolism derived from the ancient mystery wisdom with which the early Christians had to contend. The sun-aura depicted around the head of the god is reminiscent of the Christian halo. Another Mithraic survival into mediaeval symbolism was the strangely shaped initiate cap worn by Mithras.

The site is signposted from a parking area south of the B6318, north-west of Hexham. Some signs refer to 'Brocolitia', others to Carrawburgh.

Food and Drink: In Hexham at the Beaumont, Beaumont Street (0434 602331); or the Royal, Priestpopple (0434 602270).

LITTLE SALKELD

Standing stones – stone circle

Cumbria   MAP REF. NY5636

A large number of standing stones are set in a close circle near the village of Little Salkeld. Alongside is a square-section standing stone, the largest of all this group, called Long Meg. The angles of the square section are directed towards the four points of the compass. Long Meg is said to have been a witch who was petrified with her daughters for some crime, often said to be for dancing on the sabbath. Until 1962, a church service, arranged by nearby Addingham church, would be held within the circle, on the Sunday nearest to Midsummer Day, a modern shadow of the pagan rituals held there thousands of years ago.

Little Salkeld is north-east of Penrith, signposted to the east of the B6412. Meg and her daughters are signposted from the Glassonby road.

Food and Drink: In Penrith at the George, Devonshire Street (0768 62696); or Abbotsford, Wordsworth Street (0768 63940).

MAYBURGH

Standing stone – earthwork

Cumbria   MAP REF. NY5229

The earthwork at Mayburgh, Yanwath, consists of

9. *Part of the bank at Mayburgh henge*

banks, 3 metres high. Four stones were to be seen in the nineteenth century, with a further four at the entrance. Now, a single stone stands at the centre. It is a place to speculate on the nature of the original earthwork. Dowsers may enjoy working at this particular site to discover its original shape and purpose, and perhaps aspects that still remain hidden.

Yanwath is on the south-eastern outskirts of Penrith.

Food and Drink: In Penrith at Abbotsford, Wordsworth Street (0768 63940); or the George, Devonshire Street (0768 62696).

CASTLERIGG (THE KESWICK CARLES)

Stone circle – standing stones – power point

Cumbria   MAP REF. NY3024

Before considering the circle, it is worthy of comment that this location near Keswick is perhaps the most beautiful for any of the ancient sacred places in the British Isles. It is surrounded on all sides, except to the east, by a panorama of mountain peaks. The diameter of this most remarkable of stone circles, which dates from around 2000 BC, is about 30 metres, its pattern now being marked out by 38 standing stones or carles.

Ten of the 38 stones form a roughly rectangular enclosure within the main circle. This is usually referred to as the Cove. Its purpose is unknown. Archaeologists tentatively associate Castlerigg with a number of other sites in the north-west of England.

Earth mysteries researcher John Glover has described how certain stones in the circle seem to possess a curious association with parts of the skyline, visually echoing the contours of the horizon when viewed in a particular direction, as if they were subtle direction markers. In an article in *The Ley Hunter*, Glover reported an experience at the circle while preparing to photograph the midsummer sunset: 'I became more and more intent, concentrating to get the photographs I wanted, when, for no apparent reason I turned round. There at my feet was a wide, dark shadow extending for hundreds of yards in the direction of the notch marking the Candlemas rising sun. I was utterly amazed by this and my first reaction was to run down it as fast as I could; I felt projected into one of those fairytale situations when, if you are at the right place at the right time, a secret path appears to show you the way to a treasure.'

Paul Devereux, who has also made extensive studies of this site, has this to say about its use (from *Earth Memory*, a book which uses Castlerigg as an example of how to unravel the mysteries of ancient sacred sites): 'The principle use of Castlerigg today is as a site to visit. It is visually dramatic, in good condition and accessible from Keswick, so is on the tourist route. This is not to be denigrated. Making pilgrimages to ancient sites is quoted in surveys as a major motive among tourists. It is a way modern people can connect back with their earlier relationship with the land. Just being at a sacred site can impart some indefinable quality of well-being to the visitor. The second use to which Castlerigg, along with many other sites, is put is as a learning tool;

10. Castlerigg. The leaning stone on the right (the westernmost point of the circle) is magnetic and will affect a compass held next to it

a subject of study . . . This is a principle function of ancient sacred sites; they are repositories of perennial knowledge . . . The original users of Castlerigg would have been practising some version or other of shamanism', by which he means the contacting of non-ordinary realities – the spirit-world.

Signposted to the south-east of Keswick, Castlerigg (The Keswick Carles) is to the north of the A591.

Food and Drink: In Keswick at Skiddaw, Main Street (07687 72071); or Highfield, The Heads (07687 72508).

HARDKNOTT

Legend – power point – faeries

Cumbria   MAP REF. NY2402

Eveling, the king of the faeries, holds his invisible court in the ruins of the Roman fort at Hardknott, below Hardknott Pass. His daughter, Modron, who became known in French romantic literature, as Morgan la Fey, is the fairy who healed King Arthur, and persuaded Merlin to leave the world of mortals behind. Some mythologists report that she is the same as the Irish lake goddess, Murigen, who changed into a salmon. This change is a theme found in mythological stories as a symbol for reincarnation.

Hardknott is below Sca Fell, to the east of Beckfoot

in Eskdale, to the north-east of Ravensglass, to the west of Ambleside.

Food and Drink: In Ambleside at Glen Rothay, Rydal (05394 3254).

TYNWALD HILL, ST JOHN'S

Ritual – earthwork

Isle of Man   MAP REF. SC2882

Churches dedicated to St John the Baptist, whose feast day was celebrated on Midsummer Day, generally indicate that pagan Midsummer fire festivals were long ago practised there. A present-day ceremony with its roots in pagan history still takes place every 5 July, the old Midsummer Day, on the Isle of Man. A service is first held in the nearby St John's church, then the centre of attention moves to a site consisting of a four-tiered conical mound of earth. During the ceremony on Tynwald Hill, the laws passed during the previous year are read out to the audience. As the day is a national holiday, a fair is held on the green.

The village is on the A1 east of Peel where it crosses the A4.

Food and Drink: In Douglas at Sefton, Harris Promenade (0624 626011); or Woodbourne, Alexander Drive (0624 21766).

BEETHAM FAIRY STEPS

Legend

Cumbria   MAP REF. SD4979

Climb these steps without touching the walls of limestone on either side and you may make a wish that will
come true. The steps are cut into a crevice of sheer
limestone, reached by a pathway to the west of the old
church at Beetham.

Beetham is on the A6, north of Carnforth, which is
to the west of junction 35 of the M6.

Food and Drink: In Carnforth at the Royal Station,
Market Street (0524 732033).

THE SOCKBURN WURM

Legend

County Durham   MAP REF. NZ3407

The stone called the Graystone near the village of
Sockburn, marks the spot where Sir John Conyers slew
the Sockburn Wurm, a dragon of terrible repute. The
deed took place in the fourteenth century, and the
sword which Conyers used is still preserved in the
treasury of Durham Cathedral.

Signposted from the B1264, Sockburn is 10 km
south-east of Darlington.

Food and Drink: In Darlington at Stakis White Horse, Harrowgate Hill (0325 382121); or the Coachman, Victoria Road (0325 286116).

SNAPE CASTLE

Haunting

North Yorkshire MAP REF. SE2684

The ghost of Catharine Parr, last of the six wives of Henry VIII, haunts this place. Henry married Catharine Parr in 1543. She is known to have lived in the castle for a while. The ghost is described as a young girl with long fair hair, wearing a blue dress of the Tudor style.

Snape Castle is to the east of the B6268, south of Bedale.

Food and Drink: In Leeming Bar at Motel Leeming, Bedale (0677 23611); or the White Rose, Bedale (0677 22707).

MASHAM DRUID CIRCLE

Stone circle – power point – temple – magic

North Yorkshire   MAP REF. SE2280

This Druid circle, known locally as the Ilton Circle, high on the moors to the south of Masham, was in fact built by William Danby in 1820, whose interest in Neoplatonism suggests that the layout is based on esoteric geometric principles. The circle consists of a large number of outlying stones, internal altars, standing stones and recesses. It is somewhat reminiscent of Stonehenge, with its lintel bearing uprights, and measures about 30 metres in width at its widest stretch. Locals claim that the completely buried cell and the altar stone have been used in modern times for magical practices.

Masham is to the west of the A6108, north of Ripon. The circle is signposted to the south-west, off the road to Ilton.

Food and Drink: In Masham at Jervaulx Hall, Bedale (0677 60235).

BRIMHAM ROCKS

Power point – legend

North Yorkshire   MAP REF. SE2165

These remarkable outcroppings near Pateley Bridge

attract tourists mainly for their uncanny resemblances to animals and monsters. Most popular is the 'hanging rock', a boulder of some 200 tons, balancing on a point about 30 cm wide. However, from the esoteric point of view, the occultist Madame Blavatsky saw the revolving rocking stones on the summits of some of the larger rocks as copies of the divinatory or oracular rocks used by the priests of lost Atlantis.

Brimham Rocks are west of the minor road which runs from the south of the B6265, east of Pateley Bridge, towards Summer Bridge.

Food and Drink: In Ripon at the Bridge, Magdalen Road (0765 3687); or the Unicorn, Market Place (0765 2202).

THE DEVIL'S ARROWS, BOROUGHBRIDGE

Standing stones – ley – power point

North Yorkshire   MAP REF. SE3966

The three colossal stones that comprise the Devil's Arrows are over 3000 years old, and form an alignment 174 metres long. The tallest is over 6.7 metres high and the stones are monoliths of millstone grit. They may be the remnants of a more extensive arrangement as it is known that at least one upright is now missing. Lockyer held that they were part of an ancient sun-worship avenue, running on a south-to-north axis. The southernmost stone is now fenced off, almost part of a private garden. Legends claim that the

11. The tallest of the three remaining Devil's Arrows standing stones

stones are the remains of a volley shot from the Devil's bow, or that the Devil hanged himself from the tallest stone. The monoliths were fired by the Devil at the nearby town of Aldborough whose inhabitants had upset him. Fortunately, the Devil seems to have missed his mark. Whatever the origin of these stones, the earth energy that runs through them can be distinctly felt.

The stones are visible from the A1(M) to the west of Boroughbridge, which is on the B6265, north-north-west of Knaresborough.

Food and Drink: In Boroughbridge at the Crown, Horsefair (0423 322328).

ALDBOROUGH

Church — symbols

North Yorkshire MAP REF. SE4066

An image of the god Mercury, with his magical rod, the caduceus of two intertwining snakes, can be found carved in a Roman altar in the north aisle of St Andrew's church. The church is built over the ruins of a Roman temple dedicated to Mercury. Among other attributes and qualities, the messenger of the gods, Mercury (Hermes in Greek mythology), was a god of healing. He was also known to be a mischief-maker. Aldborough was originally the Roman town of Isurium Brigantum. Look also for the quatrefoil crosses on the thigh armour of a memorial brass to William de Aldborough in the north wall. The symbol is based on the magical three of the clover-leaf design.

Aldborough is signposted to the east of the B6265, which is off the A1(T) to the south of Thirsk.

Food and Drink: In Ripon at the Bridge Hotel, Magdalen Road (0765 3687); or the Unicorn, Market Place (0765 2202).

SKEWSBY MAZE

Earthwork – power point – symbols

North Yorkshire MAP REF. SE6372

Perhaps the smallest maze in Britain, the Skewsby Maze, or Brandsby Maze, as it is sometimes known, has been resited and recut. The original turf maze was recorded as being completely destroyed by the cart tracks which ran over it. Dowsers may be interested to trace the original location and check to see if the formal pattern has been reproduced accurately.

The maze is on the grass verge between Skewsby and Brandsby.

Food and Drink: In Easingwold at the George, Market Place (0347 21698).

RUDSTON

Standing stone – legend

Humberside   MAP REF. TA0967

The sheer size of this phallic standing stone makes it worth a visit. Standing 7.5 metres above the ground with a possible additional 7.5 metres below ground, the monolith situated in the churchyard at Rudston is the tallest monolithic standing stone in Britain. The church is Norman, but the stone dates back to 1600-1000 BC, and presumably marked a sacred site before the church was built. Unlike most places where the markstone has disappeared, this one would have been too much trouble to uproot. It is purported to weigh 40 tons and probably came from Cayton Bay

12. Rudston monolith

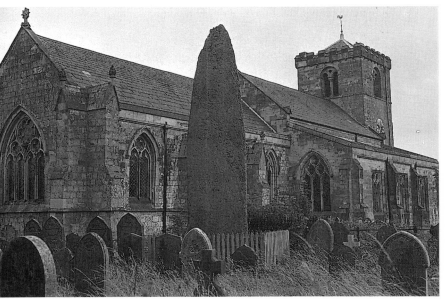

about 16 km to the north of Rudston. The Devil is supposed to have hurled the stone at the church and missed, although the stone was probably there about 4000 years before the church was built. The monolith is an axis of a nearby cursus, or straight track.

Rudston is on the B1253, west of Bridlington.

Food and Drink: In Bridlington at Monarch, South Marine Drive (0262 674447).

ALKBOROUGH MAZE

Earthwork – maze – power point – rituals

Humberside   MAP REF. SE8822

A large turf maze, called locally Julian's Bower, has been cut into a basin-shaped depression on the hillside above the village of Alkborough. It is not so much a maze as a dance pattern, for it is not possible to 'lose' oneself in the formal design. The maze can be seen as a symbol of life, into which we the dancers must go to find our way by diverse routes to a common goal, the centre of the maze. On the hilltop is an earthwork thought by some to be Roman, but it is likely to be older. In the early nineteenth century, the villagers played May Eve games in the maze. As they ran along the paths to the centre and back to the outside, one youth wrote that he had ". . . an indefinite persuasion of something unseen and unknown cooperating with them."

Alkborough is signposted to the north of Burton-upon-Stather, which is on the B1430 north of Scunthorpe.

Food and Drink: In Scunthorpe at Wortley House, Rowland Road (0724 842223).

HAWKSWORTH

Haunting

West Yorkshire   MAP REF. SE1641

Seventeenth-century Hawksworth Hall is home to three ghosts: a cowled monk, a woman who insists on opening doors and leaving them open, and the ghost of a negro page boy with the habit of leaving dirty handprints on pillows. The witchcraft king, James I, stayed here for some time, the coved ribbed plaster ceiling in the main room bearing his coat of arms.

Hawksworth is signposted off the A6038 to the west of Guiseley.

Food and Drink: In Bingley at Bankfield, Bradford Road (0274 567123).

THE SWASTIKA STONE, ILKLEY

Stone carving – power point – symbols

West Yorkshire   MAP REF. SE1147

The Swastika Stone on the edge of the Ilkley moors above the town incorporates a design probably over 3000 years old. The design only vaguely represents a swastika, but is probably more complex in form and purpose. The original design is almost obliterated by the ravages of the weather, but a copy has been placed nearby for comparison purposes. The swastika is an ancient sigil which, among other interpretations, represents the wheel of the sun as it progresses on its daily and annual journey. The word swastika is Sanskrit, meaning 'well being'. The symbol has been found in Hindu carvings, in South American rock carvings, and on Central American mound-builders' pottery.

Ilkley is on the A65, north of Bradford. The Swastika Stone is to the right of the pathway along the top of the moor, in the direction of Addingham.

13. One of the many carved stones on Rombalds Moor, near Ilkley. The Bronze Age markings shown here are nicknamed 'The Tree of Life'

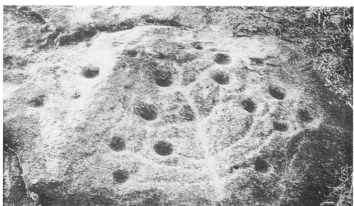

Rombald's moor is littered with carved stones and circles, for example the Pancake Stone, with its cup and ring markings and The Twelve Apostles, where three of the most important ley lines on these moors cross.

Food and Drink: In Ilkley at the Grove, 66 The Grove (0943 600298); or Sabera, Wells Road (0943 607104).

DOUBLER STONES, ADDINGHAM

Stone carvings – rituals – power point

West Yorkshire   MAP REF. SE0749

On the top surface of each of the two curiously eroded rocks called the Doubler Stones are a number of prehistoric carvings, mainly in the form of hollowed-out cups. These surfaces were allegedly used as slaughter stones by the Druids, and the cups, with their incised channels, were for collecting blood. It is probable that the stones were used for some occult religious purposes.

The Doubler Stones are approached from the west of Addingham, to the south of the A6034. The continuation of this minor road terminates at a private road leading to a farm. The rocks are visible on the skyline above the farm, to the east.

Food and Drink: In Ilkley at Rombalds, Wells Road (0943 603201); or the Grove, 66 The Grove (0943 600298).

BOLTON PRIORY GHOST

Haunting

North Yorkshire   MAP REF. SE0854

The ghost's identity is unknown, but it is that of an old man of middle height, with a heavily wrinkled and unshaven face. He wears the cowled habit of an Augustinian monk. The ghost which haunts the priory has been well documented, presumably because it has been sighted by such people as King George V, the Duke of Devonshire and Lord Desborough. In 1973, a group of amateur archaeologists also saw a ghost in mediaeval dress. At the time, they were searching for the burial place of John de Clifford, who was killed in 1461.

The priory is signposted to the north of the A59, east of Skipton.

Food and Drink: In Skipton at Tarn House, Stirton (0756 4891); or the Devonshire Arms, Bolton Abbey (0756 71441).

KEIGHLEY BUS STATION

Carved stone – power point

West Yorkshire   MAP REF. SE0540

In the unlikely occult power point of Keighley central bus station can be found a carved stone, reputed to be over 3500 years old. It was originally positioned on nearby Baildon Moor. Such incisions, the ring and cup markings, that are engraved in the stone, are likely to have been used as ancient pointers to stone circles. They are found mainly on rocks in the north of England, in Scotland and in Ireland. One theory links them with mazes, while another suggests that they were maps showing the locations of all the local sacred sites.

Keighley is on the A650, north-west of Bradford. The stone is south of North Street, almost opposite Lloyds Bank.

Food and Drink: In Keighley at Beeches, Bradford Road (0535 607227).

GIGGLESWICK

Church – astrology – symbols – holy well

North Yorkshire   MAP REF. SD8063

The images carved on the panels of the pulpit in St Alkelda's church correspond to the twelve zodiacal associations drawn up in the mediaeval period, mainly by William Durandus. The carvings, dated 1680, of the twelve sons of Jacob, each relating to a tribe of Israel, are all accompanied by an astrological image. The twelve are not in the usual astrological order.

There is a healing well to the north-east of Giggleswick. Called the Ebbing and Flowing Well, there is a nineteenth-century stained-glass window in St Alkelda's showing the spirit of the well in the form of an angel hovering above the waters. This is a Christianised version of the pagan water-sprites, called undines.

Giggleswick is signposted west of the A65, south of Settle. St Alkelda's is to the north-west of the village. The well is to the east of the A65, a few hundred metres north of the slip road to Giggleswick.

Food and Drink: In Settle at the Royal Oak, Market Place (07292 2561).

PENDLE HILL

Earthwork – zodiac – symbols – leys

Lancashire   MAP REF. SD8041

The distinctive Pendle Hill has been described as the centre for a huge earthworks zodiac. The hill also marks the convergence point of several ley lines and is probably visited most often because of the hill's associations with seventeenth-century witchcraft.

Best approached by way of the footpaths from Newchurch-in-Pendle or Berley, the hill is a distinct shape visible from many points on the A59 and the A682.

Food and Drink: In Nelson at Great Marsden, Barkerhouse Road (0282 64749).

14. The big end of Pendle Hill. George Fox, founder of the Quaker Movement, had his spiritual vision here in 1652. It was also where the Pendle Witches gathered

NEWCHURCH-IN-PENDLE

Magic – tomb – symbols

Lancashire   MAP REF. SD8239

To the south of the village church is a flat gravestone, said to mark the burial place of a local witch called Alice Nutter. The grave's inscription is worn away, but it was probably assumed to be a witch's tomb because of the grotesque carving of a face, originally a Christian death's head symbol and now much weathered. On the church's tower is a stone eye, the pupil of blue slate, the eyebrow a projecting stone. Called locally the Eye of God, it was placed there in the early sixteenth century to ward off the power of the evil eye cast by witches.

Newchurch-In-Pendle is signposted to the north of the A6068 to the north-west of Nelson.

Food and Drink: In Nelson at Great Marsden, Bar-kerhouse Road (0282 64749).

WALTON-LE-DALE

Church – magic

Lancashire   MAP REF. SD5528

The churchyard of St Leonards is the site of an attempt by Edward Kelly to raise the spirit of a dead man. The aim was to persuade the ghost to tell Kelly, and his assistant Paul Waring, the whereabouts of his considerable riches. Engravings of the event can be found in many occult books, although it is not known for sure whether or not this act of necromancy was successful.

Walton-Le-Dale is south of Preston, signposted to the south of the B6230.

Food and Drink: In Walton-Le-Dale at Vineyard, Cinnamon Hill, Chorley Road (0772 54646).

THE GODSTONE, FORMBY

Legend – symbols – ley

Merseyside   MAP REF. SD2907

Explore the churchyard of St Luke's in Formby and you will find what locals call the Godstone. This carved symbol is a combination of the calvary cross and an

Egyptian ankh, the sign of the life-force. Ancient custom describes how the newly deceased corpse would be carried around such stones to persuade the spirit to go on its journey without haunting the place. Current speculation suggests that this Godstone may be a ley marker.

Formby is on the A565(T), north-west of Liverpool.

Food and Drink: In Southport at Balmoral Lodge, Queens Road (0704 44298); or Bold, Lord Street (0704 32578).

BIDSTON HILL

Stone carvings – power point – ritual

Cheshire   MAP REF. SJ2990

A carving of what is alleged to be a sun goddess is among several figures that can be found on a flat sandstone outcrop by the Observatory on Bidston Hill. The figure, about one metre long and facing north of east, holds an object which might be a large key or cloak. At her feet is carved a symbol representing the sun. There is also a carving of a cat-headed moon goddess, with an image representing the moon at her feet. The carvings are thought to have been made by the Norse-Irish, who settled here around AD 1000, although the carvings have been renewed over the years.

Also to be found on Bidston Hill is a horse hill figure, about 3 metres long, which faces exactly towards the midsummer sunrise. Carvings of human figures are also to be found. These originated in the eighteenth century and probably represent the Mummers' Play, performed near here until recent years.

Bidston Hill is situated in Birkenhead, close to the beginning of the M53.

Food and Drink: In Birkenhead at Riverhill, Talbot Road, Oxton (051 653 3773).

IMAGES HOUSE, BUNBURY

Magic – symbols – legend

Cheshire   MAP REF. SJ5658

Various amuletic carvings are set into the brickwork or used as grotesque supports of the appropriately named Images House. The story tells how a poacher was sentenced to deportation by the squire at Bunbury, and on his return made three rough images to represent the squire and two men who had aided him. The poacher cursed the dolls each day. The story was developed in Beatrice Tonshow's novel, *Shiney Night*, but one may not doubt that the carvings were intended for magical purposes.

The Images House fronts directly on to the west side of the A49, just before the turn to Bunbury, from Northwich.

Food and Drink: In Northwich at Woodpecker, London Road (0606 45524).

SANDBACH CROSSES

Power point – symbols – monument

Cheshire   MAP REF. SJ7661

Two crosses standing in the marketplace at Sandbach were smashed by the Puritans in 1614 and the pieces used for various building purposes. They were finally collected together again and the crosses re-erected in 1816. They are elaborately sculpted with Christian religious scenes, animals, and scenes depicting the conversion to Christianity in AD 653 of Peada of Mercia. It is estimated that the crosses were erected between the seventh and ninth centuries.

The town is north-east of Crewe, to the west of the M6, junction 17.

Food and Drink: In Sandbach at Old Hall, Newcastle Road (0270 761221).

SHAROW PYRAMID

Power point – symbols – sacred architecture

North Yorkshire   MAP REF. SE3271

A miniature version of the Great Pyramid of Cheops at Giza in Egypt, can be found in the churchyard of St John's in Sharow. This gravestone was built by Charles Piazzi Smyth, famous for his pioneering work in connection with the esoteric significance and properties of the Egyptian pyramids. Smyth developed complex numerological theories, based on their structure, and revealed the astronomical orientations of the interior passageways. The inscription on the pyramid tomb is a tribute to Smyth's wife.

Sharow is signposted to the east of Ripon, off the A61.

Food and Drink: In Ripon at New Hornblower, Duck Hill (0765 4841); or the Unicorn, Market Place (0765 2202).

CENTRAL

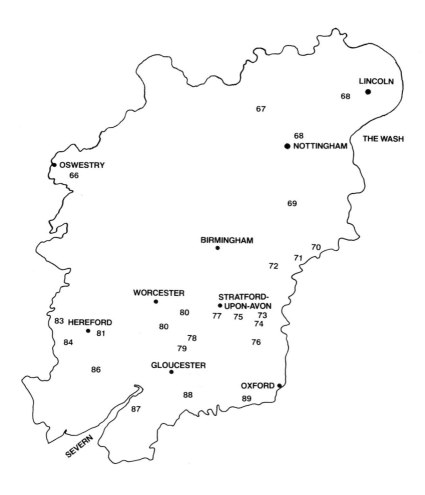

LINCOLN
68

67

68
NOTTINGHAM

THE WASH

OSWESTRY
66

69

BIRMINGHAM

70
71
72

WORCESTER

STRATFORD-
UPON-AVON

80
77   75   73
74

83 HEREFORD
80
84   81

78
79

76

86

GLOUCESTER

OXFORD
89
88

87

SEVERN

WOOLSTON

Holy well

Shropshire   MAP REF. SJ3224

A half-timbered cottage is now sited over the water flow of the healing well at Woolston. It is likely that a chapel was once built over the well whose waters were once valued for their magical powers to heal wounds and bruises. The site is a particularly beautiful one, situated in the Welsh border country.

Woolston is signposted to the west of West Felton on the A5(T), near Oswestry.

Food and Drink: In Oswestry at The Wynnstay Hotel, Church Street (0691 655261); or Sweeny Hall, Morda (0691 652450).

15. View from Woolston towards the Welsh border

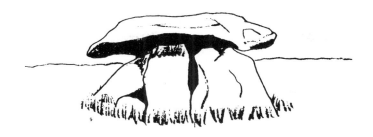

ARBOR LOW

Stone circle – burial mounds

Derbyshire   MAP REF. SK1664

All the stones in this circle, high on the Derbyshire moors, near Middleton, lie on their backs and may never have stood upright. It is said that 50 leys pass through this site. This indicates that it could have been a particularly active centre for religious, ritual, or alignment purposes. The leys are at least simple alignments of particular landmarks but as modern research has shown, they may also have a relationship with esoteric forms of earth energies. Close by the circle are burial mounds, one being part of the outer bank of the earthwork. The stones are limestone, the largest originally weighing about 10 tons.

Arbor Low is east of the A515, south of Buxton and north of the B5054 turning towards Leek.

Food and Drink: In Buxton at the Buckingham, 1 Burlington Road (0298 70481); or Nathaniels, 35 High Street (0298 78388).

KIRKLINGTON

Church – astrology – symbols

Nottinghamshire   MAP REF. SK6757

Look for the sundial on the south wall of St Swithin's church. This large twelfth-century stone is worked with occult symbols. The nine-squared grid is that linked with the planet, Saturn, for which the numerical equivalent is 45. The association is confirmed by a four-pointed star to the left, and a five-pointed star to the right. Saturn, sometimes called Chronos, was the god of time. In astrology, Saturn is the planet that brings limitations, responsibilities, and lessons in life – the planet of karma.

   Kirklington is on the A617, north-west of Southwell.

   Food and Drink: In Southwell at the Saracen's Head, Market Place (0636 812701).

THE LINCOLN IMP

Legend

Lincolnshire   MAP REF. SK9771

Inside Lincoln cathedral, high on a pillar in the Angel Choir is a dramatic grotesque known as the Lincoln Imp. This was once a real elemental creature, a troublesome demon who caused much difficulty for those building the cathedral. He was turned to stone when the priests exorcised him, to become what is probably the only petrified demon in England.

Lincoln is on the junction of the Foss Way (A46) and Ermine Street (A15).

Food and Drink: In Lincoln at the Barbican, St Mary's Street (0522 28374); or Harveys Cathedral, 1 Exchequergate, Castle Square (0522 510333).

BEACON HILL

Earthwork – legend – power point

Leicestershire   MAP REF. SK5115

Beacon Hill, near Woodhouse Eaves, is 250 metres high, and evidence of prehistoric occupation can be found in the remains of an Iron Age hillfort. The name of the hill suggests that it was once used as a beacon site. The second highest hill in the county, this excellent vantage point is haunted by the ghost of a monk. Those who have seen the ghost report a skeletal face, the figure being accompanied by a dog.

Lying to the east of the M1, the hill can be reached from junction 23, and by travelling south from Loughborough on the A6 and turning right onto the B591.

Food and Drink: In Loughborough at Great Central, Great Central Road (0509 263405).

WING MAZE

Earthwork – maze

Leicestershire   MAP REF. SK9003

Close to this maze is a large tumulus, an indicator of the maze's prehistoric origins. This particular design in the village of Wing, has been well cared for and is in an excellent state of preservation.

Take the A6003 south from Oakham, past Rutland Water, and the village of Wing is to the east of the main road.

Food and Drink: In Oakham at Boultons, Catmore Street (0572 2844); or the Rutland Angler, Mill Street (0572 55839).

16. The ancient turf labyrinth at Wing

THE TRIANGULAR LODGE, RUSHTON

Power point – folly – symbols – numerology

Northamptonshire   MAP REF. SP8482

Built in the sixteenth century, to satisfy the folly-taste of Sir Thomas Tresham, this building appears to do no more than pay homage to the Trinity: the building has three sides and three floors, and each side is topped by three triangular gables. Closer examination, however, reveals that the structure expresses numerological symbolism of a complex nature. Every number below 72 may be discovered within this building by means of numerological multiplication, reduction and extension. The dates and numbers on each of the three faces are also of considerable numerological import. For example, the date over the doorway is linked with the ancient notion of the creation of the world having taken place in 3962 BC. Visitors should refer to the HMSO guide book for information about the deeper implications of the building.

The lodge is signposted north-west of the A6(T) at Desborough. The Triangular House is in the grounds of Rushton House.

Food and Drink: In Kettering at the Periquito Hotel, Market Square (0536 520732).

BRINKLOW

Earthwork – church

Warwickshire   MAP REF. SP4480

The church at Brinklow, near Coventry, is dedicated
to St John the Baptist, whose feast day was celebrated
on Midsummer Day, indicating the possibility that
celebrations for Midsummer of a pre-Christian nature
may have taken place on the site. Significantly, the
ground rises steeply at the edge of the churchyard to
form the outside bank of a large and impressive earthwork. The Roman road, the Foss Way passes through
Brinklow, but makes a detour around the earthwork,
showing that the earthwork predates the Foss Way.

Brinklow is east of Coventry on the A4114, at its
junction with the B4029. The M6 runs to the immedi-
ate north of the town.

Food and Drink: In Coventry at Crest, Hinkley Road,
Walsgrove (0203 613261); or Hylands, Warwick Road
(0203 501600).

WARMINGTON CHURCH

Church – haunting

Warwickshire   MAP REF. SP4147

A number of soldiers slain in the battle of Edgehill
were buried in the churchyard here and the church
itself is one of many in this area said to be haunted by

these dead. The atmosphere of the churchyard is desolate and mysterious – so strangers beware.

Warmington is next to the A41(T), just north of the junction with the B4086 to Kineton.

Food and Drink: In Banbury at Cromwell Lodge, North Bar (0295 59781); or Lismore Hotel & Restaurant, 61 Oxford Road (0295 67661).

EDGEHILL

Haunting

Warwickshire   MAP REF. SP3847

Shortly after the Battle of Edgehill, which took place in October 1642, people reported seeing ghostly enactments of the battle, hearing the crash of gunfire and the sound of cavalry. The deaths of 2000 men took place in this first important battle of the civil war. The reporting officer, Colonel Sir Lewis Kirk, saw the spirit battle on two occasions, adding credence to stories from the Edgehill locals.

Edgehill is viewed best from the hamlet of Ratley, off the B4086, north-west of Banbury.

Food and Drink: In Banbury at Cromwell Lodge, North Bar (0295 59781); or Lismore Hotel and Restaurant, 61 Oxford Road (0295 67661).

17. *Initiation image carved over the south door of St Andrew's church, Great Rollright*

GREAT ROLLRIGHT

Church – hermeticism – symbols

Oxfordshire   MAP REF. SP3231

The initiation image of a man being devoured by a serpent is just one of the esoteric symbols to be found in the Norman arch over the south door of St Andrew's church in the village. This image is found in the mythology of many cultures, indicating its importance as an archetypal motif. The wall to the north of this porch has a mediaeval carving of a Green Man. This is an incongruous image to find in sanctified ground, as he is a representative of the spirit in nature and therefore a pagan symbol.

Great Rollright is signposted off the A34, north of Chipping Norton.

Food and Drink: In Stow-on-the-Wold at the Grapevine, Sheep Street (0451 30344); or Stow Lodge, The Square (0451 30485).

THE ROLLRIGHT STONES

Stone circle – standing stones – earthwork – power point

Oxfordshire   MAP REF. SP3231

The Rollright Stones form an almost perfect circle. Known also as the King's Men, the megalithic monument is perhaps the most famous of the smaller circles. As with many other such monuments, it is said that it is impossible to count the number of stones accurately. The stones are supposed to walk at midnight, and will troop to the spring in Little Rollright Spinney to drink. Those with an interest in the esoteric and in earth mysteries recognise the Rollrights as a major power point and will pilgrimage here to meditate and experience its powerful 'earth energies'. A famous legend tells that all these stones were originally a king and his men who were turned into stone by a witch.

The nearby Whispering Knights, a short distance to the south, are the upright remains of a burial chamber. The stones are still regarded as whispering oracles. Listen at a crevice and hear the future foretold.

Paul Devereux reports in *Earth Memory* that work at the Rollright Stones, under the aegis of the Dragon Project, revealed fascinating results during instrumental monitoring of the stones: 'When resources allowed, we used magnetometers, instruments which can measure very small levels of magnetic change. These revealed that sporadic, low-level changes of magnetism could occur in standing stones. At Rollright in July 1983, we found one stone in the western sector of the circle that was fluctuating quite dramatically for a few hours in the millioersted range (the scale on the machine being used). It eventually settled down and gave a completely level reading like all the stones we monitored around it. This tallied with earlier findings by independent researcher Charles Brooker, who had measured two other magnetically pulsing stones in the circle. The reasons for this effect are currently unknown.'

The stone circle is signposted to the north-east of the A44, between Chipping Norton and Moreton-in-Marsh.

Food and Drink: In Stow-on-the-Wold at Fosse Manor (0451 30345); or Grapevine, Sheep Street (0451 30344).

18. Rollright stone circle

19. St Leonard's church, Bretforton

BRETFORTON

Church – legend – symbols

Hereford and Worcester   MAP REF. SP0944

In St Leonard's Church is a mediaeval capital carved with a strange picture of a dragon devouring St Margaret. Margaret was a martyr who was confronted by a dragon while in prison. She made the sign of the cross which grew until it eventually burst a hole in the dragon's stomach and was able to escape. The story accounts for St Margaret being the patron saint of pregnant women, but many occultists see it as a thinly disguised initiation myth. Search out the 'Witch Marks', inscribed on the floor of the nearby 'The Fleece'.

Bretforton is on the B4035, east of Evesham.

Food and Drink: In Evesham at the Northwick Arms, Waterside (0386 40322); or Park View, Waterside (0386 2639).

20. Tibble Stone

TEDDINGTON HANDS

Standing stone – legend

Gloucestershire   MAP REF. SO9633

The Tibble Stone is a deeply pitted monolith which stands at Teddington Hands, east of Tewkesbury where five roads meet. The holes in the stone, said to be made by a giant's fingers, are still visible in the standing stone. Such pagan stones were often used as mark stones, and almost always lie on important ley lines. Christians would attempt to de-paganise such stones by carving crosses, or erecting wooden crosses over the top of them, as may well have been the case at Teddington Hands, a name for the old Teddington Cross.

Teddington is situated at the junction of the A435 and A438, and a minor road from Beckford, to the north. The Tibble Stone is sunk in the grass, opposite the Teddington Hands public house.

Food and Drink: In Broadway at Collin House, Collin Lane (0386 858354).

THE DEERHURST DRAGON

Legend

Gloucestershire MAP REF. SO8729

The village of Deerhurst was once haunted by a dragon which stole the local cattle for food and poisoned the inhabitants with its breath. A royal proclamation determined that whoever could kill the dragon would receive one of the crown estates in the parish. A man named Smith succeeded in drugging the monster with milk, and while it slept he beheaded it.

Deerhurst is west of the A38, itself to the west of the M5, junctions 9 or 10.

Food and Drink: In Cheltenham at Wyaston, Parabola Road (0242 516654); or the Lansdown, Lansdown Road (0242 522700).

PRIOR COURT, CALLOW END

Haunting

Hereford and Worcester   MAP REF. SO8349

Prior Court at Callow End is haunted by several ghosts. At one time, according to the historians, Owen and Sims, a box containing a book on black magic, and what might well have been an invocator's ritual knife, were found in a hole in the rafters. It was also recounted that a skeleton in the dress of a seventeenth-century cavalier was found lodged in one of the great chimneys of a bedroom. The ghost, which has been seen most clearly, is taken to be that of a young Victorian girl, wearing a straw hat, and with her hair gathered up in a bun.

Callow End is on the B4424, south of Worcester.

Food and Drink: In Worcester at Star, Foregate Street (0905 24308); or Ye Olde Talbot, Friar Street (0905 23573).

BOSBURY MARK-STONE

Standing stone – power point

Hereford and Worcester   MAP REF. SO6943

A pagan mark-stone was discovered beneath a church-yard cross in Bosbury church, when the cross was removed from its ancient site in 1796. It was the opinion of Alfred Watkins that the huge boulder thus

21. Bosbury mark-stone lies unobtrusively at the foot of the church tower, beneath the clock

discovered was an old mark-stone. The stone is held to be sacred and may be seen today under the church tower.

Bosbury is on the B4220, north of Ledbury.

Food and Drink: In Ledbury at the Royal Oak, The Southend (0531 2110); or Verzons, Trumpet (0531 83381).

DINEDOR

Earthwork – ley lines

Hereford and Worcester   MAP REF. SO5336

An ancient earthwork encampment lies above the

small village of Dinedor, particularly significant as part of a series of alignments which are visible to the naked eye. The ley line from the eastern end of the encampment is aligned to give a view of the tower of Hereford Cathedral, centred directly on the spire of All Saint's Church. Alfred Watkins was the first to point out this alignment.

The village is signposted to the west of the B4399, south of Hereford. The camp is approached by a track to the south of the village.

Food and Drink: In Hereford at Litchfield Lodge, Bodenham Road (0432 273258); or Merton, Commercial Road (0432 265925).

22. Telephoto view south across Hereford. The spire belongs to All Saints church, and the tower to the cathedral. Alfred Watkins noted that these aligned to the prehistoric earthworks on Dinedore Hill (the tree clump on the horizon)

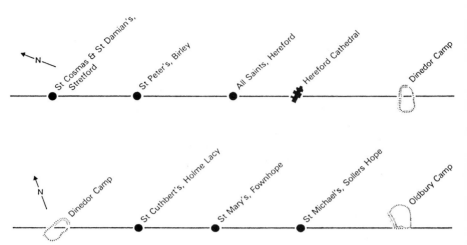

23. *Two ley lines related to Dinedoor Hill (courtesy Paul Devereux and Ian Thomson)*

ARTHUR'S STONE, DORSTONE

Burial site – ley lines

Hereford and Worcester   MAP REF. SD3141

Recorded in his classic book on the subject of ley lines, *The Old Straight Track,* by Alfred Watkins, Arthur's Stone is associated with three ley lines, one of which lies along the approach road from the east. Arthur's Stone is the name given to a megalithic burial site, known to date from around 3000 BC, on the summit of the hill to the north of Dorstone. The name originally applied only to the huge capstone, now split into two sections. Note the ley which aligns Arthur's Stone with Dorstone Church, two kilometres distant, and an elevation point above Bredwardine to the north. Dorstone is situated on the B4348 to the east of Hay-on-Wye.

24. Arthur's Stone

Arthur's Stone is signposted up a narrow road, north of the A4348, to the east of Hay-on-Wye.

Food and Drink: In Hay-on-Wye at Olde Black Lion, Lion Street (0497 820841); or Lions Corner House, Market Street (0497 820175).

KILPECK

Astrology – esoteric symbols – church

Hereford and Worcester   MAP REF. SO4430

One of the finest examples of Norman stonework to be found in a small church in Britain can be observed at the church of Sts Mary and David at Kilpeck. Particularly interesting from an occult point of view are

25. Carvings over the door of Kilpeck church

the demonic grotesques in the lower register of the tympanum arch, the astrological symbol of the Pisces image in the upper register, the orouboros (a serpent endlessly devouring its own tale), the pagan Green Man, and the strange pair of fishes to the north of the church. Look also for the Tree of Life carved on the South Doorway, and also a representation of the Sheila-na-gig, a fertility symbol in the frieze around the outside of the church.

The symbolism of the door may relate to the temptation and fall in Eden, but the real root of the symbolism is probably pagan in origin. For example, the Phrygian cap worn by one of the sculped men derives from the cult of Mithras.

Kilpeck is signposted to the south of the A465(T), south-west of Hereford.

Food and Drink: In Hereford at Castle Pool, Castle Street (0432 56321); or Graftonbury Hotel, Grafton Lane (0432 356411).

85

STAUNTON

Standing stone

Gloucestershire   MAP REF. SO5412

The Forest of Dean is host to several standing stones, such as the Staunton Stone, just outside the village of Staunton. The Buckstone above Staunton is associated with many myths including its use by Druids as an altar and by witches for their sabbats. The Buckstone, originally rather precariously pivoted, was knocked off its perch in 1885. Eventually the pieces were rebuilt on its old site, though after this reworking it no longer rocks. Locals refer to it as the Frog Stone as it looks like the bulging eye of a frog. Just above the Buckstone is the so-called Sacrificial Stone, and about 2 km to the north stands the Suck Stone.

26. Staunton Stone

Staunton is on the A4136 to the east of Monmouth. The Staunton Stone stands on the road to the east of the village. To find the Buckstone, take the small road to the left of the Post Office and continue upwards, keeping right until you are below the covered reservoir. A trackway then ascends directly to the stone.

Food and Drink: In Monmouth at the Kings Head, Agincourt Square (0600 2177); or Talocher Farmhouse, Wonastow Road (060083 236).

THE WITCH OF BERKELEY

Witchcraft – legend

Gloucestershire   MAP REF. ST6899

The Poet Laureate, Robert Southey (1774-1843), recorded the tale of the witch of Berkeley who probably lived in the ninth century. To preserve her from the Devil on her death, the witch asked that, 'When I am dead, sew my body in the hide of a stag, place it in a sarcophagus of stone, which make fast with iron and molten lead, binding around the stone three iron chains of the stoutest. Let fifty chantry priests sing a dirge for my soul . . . and if I lie for three nights in peace unharmed, on the fourth day ye shall bury me in the ground.' It didn't work. The Devil carried her off anyway, accompanied by her shrieks of agony.

Berkeley is signposted off junction 14 of the M5.

Food and Drink: In Berkeley at the Berkeley Arms, Canonbury Street (0453 810291); or Old Schoolhouse, Canonbury Street (0453 811711).

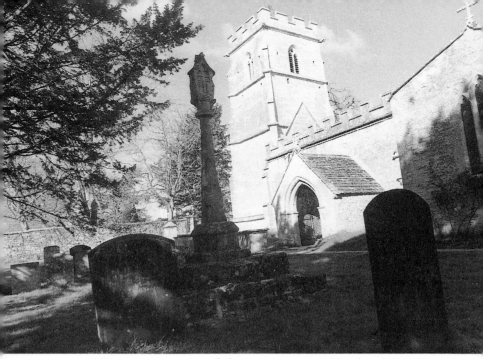

27. Ampney Crucis and the 'weeping cross'. The church has the rare dedication of the Holy Cross.

AMPNEY CRUCIS

Monument – ritual

Gloucestershire   MAP REF. SP0702

Standing in the village churchyard is a strange stone erection which was probably a 'weeping cross', a 'place to which penitents resorted to bemoan over their shortcomings.' The head of the erection was found in some rubble in the rood loft of the church, and replaced in 1860. It had probably been removed and hidden to avoid destruction by the Puritans.

The village lies east of Cirencester on the A417 to Fairford.

Food and Drink: In Cirencester at Corinium Court, Gloucester Street (0285 69711); or the King's Head, Market Place (0285 653322).

THE WHITE HORSE OF UFFINGTON

Hill figure – legend

Oxfordshire   MAP REF. SU3089

This chalk cut figure is probably the oldest of its kind in Britain. Archaeologists date it to before the 9th century, but it may be a reworking of an even older figure. The surrounding landscape is dotted with prehistoric remains, such as the megalithic burial chamber, known as Wayland's Smithy, the hill fort called Uffington Castle and the prehistoric Ridgeway.

It has been argued that the horse is actually a dragon, which may have become a horse during numerous restoration programmes. It is likely that the dragon-horse was once a sort of tribal totem. Look for the nearby Dragon's Hill top. Legend has it that this is where St George slew the Dragon. The blood pouring from the dying dragon is supposed to have caused the grass to die and the chalk outline to appear. Traditionally, every seven years at Whitsuntide, the chalk outline of the figure was cleared of grass and weeds by local villagers, and this was accompanied by games and a fair, held inside the enclosure. Today, repair work is done by the department of the environment. The angle of the slope on which the figure is cut is worthy of note - it makes the shape of the figure difficult to see from the ground, but from the air it stands out clearly.

The White Horse is best seen from the B4507.

Food and Drink: In Cirencester at Stratton House, Gloucester Road (0285 61761); or Corinium Court, Gloucester Street (0285 69711).

28. White Horse of Uffington is located top right with the Uffington Castle hill fort to the left

WALES

NORTH WALES

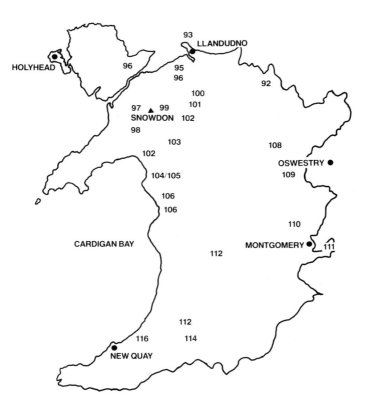

HOLYHEAD

93
LLANDUDNO

96

95
96

92

100
101

97 ▲ 99
SNOWDON 102

98

103

108

102

OSWESTRY ●

104/105

109

106
106

110

CARDIGAN BAY

MONTGOMERY ● 111

112

112

116 114

NEW QUAY

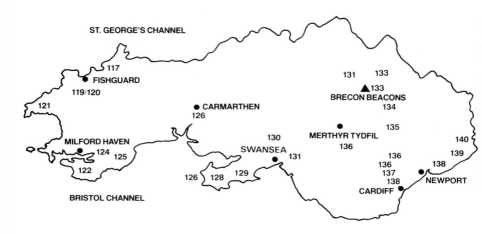

HOLYWELL

Holy well – power point

Clwyd   MAP REF. SJ1875

St Winifride's Well in the town of Holywell, was probably the best known of all Welsh healing wells, with an
output of over 20 tons of water a minute. It is today a
beautifully preserved example of a mediaeval holy
well – probably one of the best examples in Britain.
The shrine of this well has an unbroken history of
pilgrimage from the seventh century. Subject of a
poem by Gerard Manley Hopkins, the water source

29. *St Winifrede's Well, Holywell*

emerges in a mediaeval stepped cistern, surrounded by a beautiful pillared walk. This water cistern has steps to permit pilgrims total immersion. It was once customary for pilgrims to pass through the inner well three times.

Holywell is signposted to the south of the A55(T), west of Chester.

Food and Drink: In Holywell at Stamford Gate, Halkyn Road (0352 712942).

GREAT ORMES HEAD

Power point – legend – church

Gwynedd   MAP REF. SH7584

A large rocking stone, the Maen Sigl or St Tudno's Cradle was used as a magical whetstone. The stone was

93

30. Llandudno from the Great Orme

owned by Tudno, who, according to Welsh legends
was one of the survivors of the drowned country of
Cantre-y-Gwaelod, which, until the fifth century, was
on dry land in the middle of what is now Cardigan Bay.
It is likely that the church of St Tudno on the Great
Orme was built over a simple cell founded by the saint
himself. The proximity of several healing wells to the
church suggests that this used to be a centre of great
religious significance.

Great Ormes Head is to the north of Llandudno.
The pathway to the rocking stone is not signposted, so
it is advisable to ask for directions from locals. The
stone may be identified by a rectangular incision where
there was once an inscription plate.

94

Food and Drink: In Llandudno at Bedford, Promenade (0492 76647); or Merrion, South Parade (0492 860022); Royal, Church Walk (0492 76476).

PENMAENMAWR – THE DRUID'S CIRCLE

Stone circle – legend – witchcraft

Gwynedd   MAP REF. SH7176

There is an impressive megalithic stone circle on the moors above Penmaenmawr, called Y Meini Hirion, which means 'The Druid's Circle'. Within the circle is an upright which has a cavity on its top surface. Ominously called the 'sacrificial stone', it is said that a newborn child placed in the cavity will have good fortune for the rest of his or her life. This stone is, however, also associated with the rites of witchcraft. Some say that at one sabbat the noises of sobbing which came from the stone drove away most of the witches, though one was literally frightened to death, and another went mad with fear.

Penmaenmawr is on the A55(T) coast road. Directions to the site, reached by a difficult trackway are best obtained locally, otherwise use an OS map.

Food and Drink: In Bangor at the Railway, High Street (0248 362158); or Telford, Holyhead Road (0248 352543).

ROEWEN CROMLECH

Earthwork – standing stone –legend

Gwynedd   MAP REF. SH7572

Called locally the Greyhound's Kennel, the Maen y Bardd cromlech lies west of Roewen. The name is probably associated with a standing stone about 1 km to the east. A giant's dog, which had been sent to bring sheep from Tal-y-Fan, sheltered instead in the cromlech. Its giant owner was standing on Pen-y-Gaer, and in anger at the dog's disobedience, he threw the stone at the dog. The stone missed and stood almost upright in the earth, in the position which it still holds. The stone is sometimes referred to as Arthur's Spear, linking it in legend with one of the deeds of King Arthur.

Single track roads make it advisable to leave vehicles at Roewen. The Maen is to the north side of the Roman road below Tal-y-Fan, 2½ km west of Roewen, itself signposted to the west of the B5106.

Food and Drink: In Llanrwst at Eagles (0492 640454); or Meadowsweet, Station Road (0492 640732).

THE THREE LEAPS STONES, PENTRAETH

Standing stones – legend

Gwynedd   MAP REF. SH5378

Three stones in a field half a mile from Pentraeth, near

the entrance to Plas Gwyn, mark the place where a strange contest is supposed to have taken place in the sixth century. The affections of the daughter of Einim, son of St Geraint, were sought by two men, Hywel, son of Gwalchmai and another local man. The matter was to be decided by a jumping contest, to consist of three leaps. Hywel won by using a hop, skip and jump technique, enabling him to cover about 15 metres. The three stones mark the length of each leap.

The Three Leaps Stones can be found at Pentraeth, just off the A5025.

Food and Drink: In Bangor at the Railway, High Street (0248 362158); or the Telford, Holyhead Road (0248 352543).

LLYN DYWARCHEN

Legend

Gwynedd   MAP REF. SH5652

The lake of Lyn Dywarchen is associated in Welsh mythology with floating islands. The island, which 'belonged neither to the earth nor to the waters,' was said to be the meeting place of a man who had married a fairy, who, on her return to the lake, was condemned never to walk the earth again. Giraldus of Wales wrote of a floating island, which was wind carried from side to side on the lake, a phenomenon which has been observed as late as the eighteenth century. The lake certainly possesses an air of mystery.

Llyn Dywarchen is in the Nantle Valley. Take the

B4418 from Rhyd-Ddu; the lake is visible to the left, from a depression in the wood, about 1 km from the village.

Food and Drink: In Caernarfon at Menai Bank, North Road (0286 673297).

LLYN DINAS

Legend

Gwynedd   MAP REF. SH6149

From this lake can be seen the ruined castle walls of Dinas Emrys, a site linked in mythology with the origin of the emblematic Red Dragon of Wales. During the course of rebuilding the hill fort at Dinas Emrys, it was necessary to drain an underground lake to awaken two sleeping dragons who then fought to the death. According to the prophecy of a magician, perhaps Merlin himself, the Red Dragon killed the White Dragon. The lake used to be called Llyn Dinas Emrys, a reminder that one of the names of Merlin was Emrys.

Llyn Dinas is a lake of the River Glaslyn, about 3 km north-east of Beddgelert, south of the A498.

Food and Drink: In Betws-y-Coed at Park Hill, Llanrwst Road (06902 540); or Ty Gwyn (06902 383).

31. Llyn Dinas, Snowdonia

RAIADR-Y-WENNOL

Haunting – legend

Gwynedd   MAP REF. SH7956

Raiadr-y-Wennol is Welsh for the 'Swallow Falls', originally Rhaiadr Ewynol, or Foaming Falls. A story persists that the waters are haunted by an evil man. It is said that there was a hermit cell on the site of the present church of St Michael in Betws-y-Coed, while local myths of the dragon called the Wybrant Viper, give this locality an air of mystery and mythical presence.

The falls are located on the A5(T) to the west of Betws-y-Coed.

Food and Drink: In Betws-y-Coed at Park Hill, Llantwst Road (06902 540); or Ty Gwyn (06902 383).

32. Raiadr-y-Wennol

THE FOUR STONES, GWYTHERIN CHURCHYARD

Standing stones

Clwyd   MAP REF. SH8862

This is a prehistoric alignment of four stones with one bearing a fifth-century inscription commemorating Vinnemaglus, son of Sennemaglus. Stone alignments are quite rare in Wales, but this is one of the most interesting examples.

Take the A548 from Abergele south to Llanrevst, then turn onto the A544 to Llansannon, and west on the B5384, a mountain road to Gwytherin.

Food and Drink: In Abergele at Kinmel Manor, St Georges Road (0745 832014).

CAPEL GARMON

Burial chamber

Clwyd   MAP REF. SH8254

The site of the Capel Garmon burial chamber is quite high up, with a clear view of the surrounding countryside. This is a common factor among many such ancient burial chambers. This particular one has lost part of its covering mound of earth or stones and thus the details of its construction can be examined with ease.

The hill lies south of Llanrwst and is skirted by the A470(T) to the west and B5113 to the east. Betws-y-Coed is in the valley beneath the hill.

Food and Drink: In Betws-y-Coed at Park Hill, Llanrwst Road (06902 540); or Ty Gwyn (06902 383).

33. View towards Betws-y-Coed

101

PENMACHNO

Gravestone

Gwynedd MAP REF. SH7951

Originally found in a field near Penmachno, this fifth-century gravestone stands now in the grounds of the parish church. It bears a chi-rho monogram, the first letters of the Greek *Christos*, or Christ, one of very few examples in Britain. The inscription reads: CARAUSIS/HIC IACIT/IN HOC CON/GERIES LA/PIDUM. 'Here lies Carausius in this heap of stones.'

Penmachno is south-east of Betws-y-Coed on the B4406 which joins the A5(T) at Conwy Falls.

Food and Drink: In Betws-y-Coed at Park Hill, Llanrwst Road (06902 540); Ty Gwyn (06902 383).

THE FIFTEEN STONES, BRYN CADER FAWR

Stone circle – burial chamber

Gwynedd MAP REF. SH6535

To the west of Moel Ysgyfarnogod, on a rocky slope is a circle of standing stones that would originally have consisted of more than the present 15. The rectangular hole at its centre was probably a burial chamber. These were lined with stone slabs and sometimes made from hollowed tree-trunks. 'The Fifteen Stones' is located near Llandecwyn.

Travelling south from Blaenau-Ffestiniog on the A496 towards Harlech, turn left towards Llandecwyn beyond Maentwrog.

Food and Drink: In Talsarnau at Maes-y-Neuadd (0766 780200); or Tregwylan (0766 770424).

THE PULPIT STONE, FFESTINIOG

Power point – legend – magic – ritual

Gwynedd   MAP REF. SH7141

Huw Lloyd's Pulpit Stone, the highest point of which is about six metres above the waters of the Cynfal in the valley below Ffestiniog, is associated with rituals calling upon the shades of the dead. The column of natural stone closely resembles a pulpit and tradition has it that it was used in the seventeenth century by a wizard called Huw Lloyd who would curse all who crossed him. Shortly before he died, all his demonological books were thrown into Llyn Pont Rhydden, only to be caught by a mystery hand that rose from the surface and took the books.

Ffestiniog is located at the junction of the B4391 and the A470(T). The pulpit is approached by a signposted trackway to the left of the chapel just south of Ffestiniog.

Food and Drink: In Porthmadog at the Royal Sportsman, High Street (0766 2015); or Tyddyn Llwyn, Black Rock Road (0766 3903).

DYFFRYN

Standing stone

West Glamorgan   MAP REF. SS8593

Three upright stones and a capstone measuring 4.3 x 3 metres comprise a cromlech near Dyffryn in St Lythan's parish. It is purported that the huge capstone spins three times on its centre on Midsummer Eve. In his book, *Mysterious Wales*, Chris Barber records that the land in which the cromlech is found is known as the 'Accursed Field', and mentions the belief that nothing will grow in it.

Dyffryn is located to the west of the A4063, east of Neath. The cromlech is 1 km south-east of Dyffryn House.

34. One of the two surviving Dyffren dolmens. The site is located on the Mochras geological fault

Food and Drink: In Neath at Glyn Clydach, Longford Road, Neath Abbey (0792 813701); or Oak Tree Parc, Birchgrove Road (0792 817781).

CARNEDDAU HENGWM

Burial mounds

Gwynedd   MAP REF. SH6121

About 5 miles north of Barmouth, on a hillside above the A496 can be found a group of huge burial mounds. Although massive, the cairns are difficult to locate from a distance as there are so many stone walls in this area – they are situated just south of Afon Egryn. Dating back to the Neolithic Age, the northern cairn is about 30 metres long and 15 metres wide. The southern cairn would originally have been about 60 metres long and 20 metres wide and near its centre is a chamber covered by a large capstone. There is access to this by a narrow passage on the north side. The remnants of a third chamber can also be found and there is evidence of at least two other small side chambers.

Take the A496 north from Barmouth to Harlech.

Food and Drink: In Barmouth at Bryn Melyn, Panorama Road (0341 280556).

LLYN CYNWCH

Legend

Gwynedd   MAP REF. SH6521

A cairn called Carnedd-y-Wiber, Cairn of the Serpent, still marks the spot where a wild dragon was killed by a shepherd, who chanced to find it sleeping and cut off its head. The dragon inhabited the waters of Llyn Cynwch and did not kill in the usual way, for it had a basilisk eye, and could paralyse with its glance.

Llyn Cynwch is below the Precipice Walk, east of Llanelltyd, north of the A494(T).

Food and Drink: In Dolgellau at Dolserau Hall (0341 422522); or the Royal Ship (0341 422209).

CADER IDRIS

Power point – legend – UFOs

Gwynedd   MAP REF. SH7013

Few mountains have been swathed in as many legends as Cader Idris. The widely held idea that this is a place of fairies appears to stretch back beyond recorded history. The lake, Llyn Cau, near the summit of the Cader, is said to be the haunt of a sea monster, which emerges only to devour those who swim in its sacred waters. To the south of the Cadair is a crag called The Rock of the Evil One, where the Devil danced wildly in

35. *Cader Idris and Llyn Cau*

celebration of the evil ways of those who lived in Llanfihangel-y-pennant, to the south of the Cadair. The notion that anyone who sleeps on the summit of the mountain – that is on the Craig Lwyd – will be dead, a madman or a poet by morning, was probably invented by a Mrs Hemans, a romantic fiction-writer of the 19th century. Another tradition is that strange lights can be seen at the Celtic New Year.

Cader Idris is south of Dolgelau, to the west of the A487.

Food and Drink: In Dolgelau at Dolserau Hall (0341 422522); or the Royal Ship (0341 422209).

36. Moel ty Uchaf stone circle, Llandrillo

LLANDRILLO STONE CIRCLE

Stone circle – burial mound

Gwynedd   MAP REF. SJ0637

A Bronze Age stone circle with a burial mound at its centre can be found about one and a half miles north-east of Llandrillo. The circle is almost perfect in its form, with 41 stones in a circle of 11 metres in diameter.

While in this area, find the Tyfos farmhouse (Map Ref. SJ0339). Few householders can claim to have a prehistoric stone circle in their gardens – but this farmhouse boasts 14 large boulders which form a circle around a raised platform of ground.

Turn south off the A5(T) from Llangollen to Betws-y-Coed at Corwen, taking the B4401 along the valley to Llandrillo.

Food and Drink: In Llangollen at the Royal, Bridge Street (0978 860202); or Caesar's, By-the-Bridge, Castle Street(0978 860133).

PISTYLL RHAEADR

Legend

Powys   MAP REF. SJ0830

The spectacular waterfall of Pistyll Rhaeadr, the highest in Wales, was once the bathing haunt of a winged serpent who would visit nearby Llanrhaeadr-ym-Mochnant to claim its human meals. To kill the beast, a stone pillar studded with iron spikes and draped with a

37. Pistyll Rhaeadr

scarlet cloth was erected. The serpent, infuriated by the colour of the cloth, impaled itself in its anger and eventually died through loss of blood.

Pistyll Rhaeadr is north-west of Llanrhaeadr-ym-Mochnant, at the western end of the B4396.

Food and Drink: In Oswestry at Sweeney Hall, Morda (0691 652450).

MAEN LLOG, WELSHPOOL

Standing stone – legend

Powys   MAP REF. SJ2308

This large hunk of stone now stands in the graveyard of St Mary's Church, Welshpool. After the Dissolution of the monasteries, in the reign of Henry VIII, the stone stood in the church itself. Folk who were required to do penance were made to stand on the stone, dressed in a white sheet, with a candle in one hand. The Puritan, Vovasour Powel, had the stone removed from the church because he considered it an object of superstition. Before the Dissolution, the stone is reputed to have stood formerly in the abbey of Strata Marcella, where the abbots were installed on it as part of a well-established ritual. On its transference to the graveyard, the stone became a wishing stone. People would climb on it and turn around three times to face the sun and make their wish.

Welshpool stands on the River Severn, north of Montgomery and 19 miles west of Shrewsbury on the A458(T).

Food and Drink: In Welshpool at Royal Oak (0938 2217); Garte Derwen, Buttington (093874 238).

THE HYSSINGTON BULL

Legend

Powys   MAP REF. SO3194

It is probably the bull of Mithras, the god associated with the pagan cult, which was the source for the Hyssington story, which tells how, in the early days of the Christian faith, a monstrous bull terrorised the countryside around the village until a priest dealt with it. He did this by making the bull grow smaller and smaller, until it was so tiny that he could pick it up in his fingers, and drop it into his shoe. The priest then buried shoe and bull beneath the church threshold, where they still lie. The cult of Mithras, popular among the Roman legions, was involved with astrological imagery, and its rituals revolved around the annual sacrifice of the Mithraic bull. The story of the Hyssington Bull may represent the way in which the Christian religion clashed with the ancient paganism.

Hyssington is signposted to the west of the A488, south-east of Shrewsbury.

Food and Drink: In Shrewsbury at the Lion and Pheasant, Wyle Cop (0743 236288); or the Old Police House, Castle Court, off Castle Street (0743 60668).

CERRIG GAERALL CIRCLES

Stone circles

Powys   MAP REF. SH9001

East of Cemmaes and to the south of Llanbrynmair on Newydd Fynyddog Hill can be found two stone circles, about 150 metres apart. One is called Cerrig Gaerall and is 21 metres in diameter with just eight stones still standing. The other circle, called Lled Craenh yr ych, translated as 'the width of the skin of the ox', has a diameter of about 25 metres and there are only three stones left, out of an estimated original number of 15. Another stone can be found about 30 metres away from the circle.

Leave the A470(T) running north from Caersus at Llanbrynmair, and follow the B4518 which heads south towards Llanidloes.

Food and Drink: In Machynlleth at Plas Dolguog (0654 702244); or the Wynnstay Arms, Maengwyn Street (0654 2941).

DEVIL'S BRIDGE

Legend

Dyfed   MAP REF. SN7376

The lowest span of the triple-span bridge over the waterfall gorge of the Mynach was almost certainly

38. Rugged terrain near Dylife

built by the Cistercian monks of the Strata Florida
Abbey, during the eleventh century. Legend has it
though that this lowest span was built by the Devil,
tricked into doing so with the promise of a soul to take.
The Devil was to claim the first soul to cross the bridge
after its completion. However, the old woman who
made the pact threw a stick across for her dog to chase,
whose soul was then impounded, in place of that of the
old woman. Below the bridge is the gorge of the
Mynach, which swirls through the black rock swirlhole
of the Devil's Punch-bowl.

Devil's Bridge is at the junction of the A120, the
B4343 and the B4574, to the east of Aberystwyth.

Food and Drink: In Llanidloes at the Red Lion,
Longbridge Street (05512 2270).

113

39. Devil's Bridge

STRATA FLORIDA

Symbols – legend

Dyfed   MAP REF. SN7465

Little remains of the once magnificent abbey, in the midst of this wild region of central Wales. At one time the Cistercian monks held in their charge the Nanteos Chalice (Welsh, Cwpan) said to have been carved from the wood of the calvary cross. It is claimed by some that this is the chalice of the Grail legends. Whatever its origin, the cup held great healing properties, passed to

40. Strata Florida

those who drank from it. The remains of the cup still exist, although its current whereabouts is unknown. The southerly line of old chapels at Strata Florida are paved with mediaeval titles, depicting esoteric symbols.

The abbey is signposted to the east of the B4343, to the south of Devil's Bridge.

Food and Drink: In Aberystwyth at Belle Vue Royal, Marine Terrace (0970 617558); or Cambrian, Alexandra Road (0970 612446).

GARREG Y BIG, NEAR CROSS INN

Standing stone – legend

Dyfed   MAP REF. SN5465

In the mist, this standing stone can look like a gigantic figure wrapped in a grey cloak. A local story describes how the stone was carried by the Devil from the top of Trichrug Mountain when he was building the famous Devil's Bridge across the Afon Mynach. The stone was very heavy so he sat down to rest a while. Startled by the sudden crowing of a cockerel, he jumped up and fled, leaving the stone behind. You can see why the Devil needed a rest, as even today the stone stands over 4 metres high and nearly 3 metres in diameter at its base.

Cross Inn is east of Aberaeron on the B4577 where it bisects the B4337.

116

Food and Drink: In New Quay at the Black Lion
(0545 560209).

NEVERN

Church – legend – symbols

Dyfed   MAP REF. SN0840

Look for the bleeding tree in the avenue of yew trees in
the churchyard at Nevern. It is said that the 'blood' will
drip until the day that Nevern Castle is in the hands of
a Welshman. Virtually nothing exists of the castle
today, although the said tree does bleed a red, resinous
discharge.

The site was founded by St Brynach, a Celtic holy
man, who spoke with the angels on Carnbagh (visible

41. Nevern church

42. Nevern cross

43 Bleeding Yew

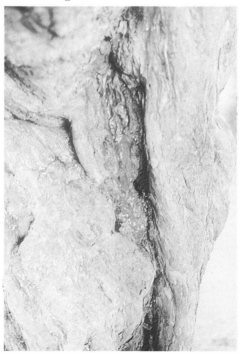

118

from the church). This hilltop has a reversed magnetic field – compass needles turn round!

Also in the churchyard is a fine example of a Celtic cross, over 3½ metres high, its surface adorned with interlace designs, symbolic forms and Nordic inscriptions.

Nevern is on the B4582, west of Cardigan. The 'bleeding tree' is the second yew on the right as you walk towards the church porch.

Food and Drink: In Cardigan at the Black Lion, High Street (0239 612532).

PARC Y MEIRW

Standing stones – legend

Dyfed   MAP REF. SM9936

Parc y Meirw means 'Field of the Dead' and here can be seen an impressive row of eight stones, four of which are still standing. The row covers a distance of 40 metres and stories are told of a ghostly lady in white being seen in the vicinity.

Take the B4313 south-east of Fishguard towards Pontfaen.

Food and Drink: In Fishguard at Cartref, High Street (0348 872430); Manor House, Main Street (0348 873260).

PENTRE IFAN

Standing stones – megalithic tomb – legend

Dyfed   MAP REF. SN0937

Probably the most famous megalithic tomb in Wales, Pentre Ifan is associated even today as a place where the fairies gather. In earlier times it was called Coetan Arthur (Arthur's Quoit) and has a mystical air by virtue of the narrow points of the three upright stones which bear the capstone at the tomb's 'open' end. The impression given is that the capstone is actually floating. The word 'cromlech' was first used in connection with this tomb by the historian George Owen in the

44. Pentre Ifan burial chamber

sixteenth century. Called cromlechs or quoits or dolmens, such arrangements of massive slabs of stone, which are thought to be the remains of ancient burial chambers, were perhaps originally covered by barrows of earth or cairns of stones.

Pentre Ifan is signposted down a series of narrow lanes to the south of the A487(T), to the east of Fishguard.

Food and Drink: In Fishguard at Cartref, High Street (0348 872430); or Abergwaun, Market Square (0348 872077).

ST DAVID'S CATHEDRAL

Astrology – church – symbols – holy well

Dyfed   MAP REF. SM7525

Look for the Abraham stone set in the wall of the south transept, the oldest part of the existing cathedral. Note the alpha and omega sigils on either side of the topmost cross and also the interlaced encircled cross. There is reference to the Taurean bull in the lower part of the design and the astrological theme is continued in the nearby chapel of Edward the Confessor. A sculptor has here worked the symbols of the four evangelists in a manner directly associated with their Babylonian origin.

While in St David's, visit St Non's Well, whose healing waters work most efficaciously on St David's Day. The stone structure of the well still preserves the seats where people would be placed in the hope of curing their various ills.

St David's is at a westerly curve of the A487, west of Haverfordwest. St Non's well is 2 km south of St David's.

Food and Drink: In St David's at the Grove, High Street (0437 720341); or the Old Cross, Cross Square (0437 720387).

45. St. David's cathedral

ST GOVAN'S CHAPEL

Chapel – legend – holy well

Dyfed   MAP REF. SR9792

Many of the fitments of this tiny chapel are cut from solid rock, and some are ascribed magical properties.

46. St. Goran's chapel

The chapel itself is wedged into the crevice end of a mass of rocks within a steep-sided crevice to the west of St Govan's Head. The chapel was probably built in the thirteenth century, but the altar, said to be the tomb of St Govan, and a seat cut into the rock wall are much earlier constructions. Tradition has it that it is not possible to count the steps leading from the cliff-top through the chapel and down to the sea. The external healing well, recently restored just below the chapel, was probably the reason why a chapel was built in this remote place. There is a legend that the chapel bell was stolen by pirates, but the undines took it back. They hid it in a rock which is supposed to ring when struck. The problem is, which rock is it?

The chapel is to the south of Bosherston, which is signposted to the south of the B4319, south of Pembroke.

Food and Drink: In Pembroke at the Coach House Inn, Main Street (0646 684602); or Holyland, Holyland Road (0646 681444).

CAREW CROSS

Stone carving – symbols – Celtic cross

Dyfed   MAP REF. SN0504

Said to be the finest sixth-century Celtic cross in Britain, this beautifully carved cross is well preserved and reveals a variety of designs, typical of Celtic patterns. On the top panel, beneath the head of the cross, is the swastika, a sun symbol, while beneath this is an intricate, interwoven ribbon pattern, without any ends. If the ribbon is traced, from wherever you start then you will be returned eventually to that point. This fact is not apparent by casual observation and perhaps is symbolic of life itself – by circuitous and unknown means, we eventually return to the point of our source. The cross stands on a specially constructed stone. An

47. Carew Cross

ancient carved inscription on the back of the stone indicates that it was used – long after it had been carved – to commemorate King Mariteut, who ruled over south-west Wales in the 11th century.

Carew is situated at the junction of the A477(T) Saundersfoot to Pembroke Dock road and the A4075 northbound route.

Food and Drink: In Pembroke at Holyland, Holyland Road (0646 681444); or Underdown Country House, Grove Hill (0646 683350).

CALDEY ISLAND

Stone carvings – power point – symbols

Dyfed MAP REF. SS1496

The Ogham stone on the small monastic Caldey Island is found within the boundaries of the church of St Illtud. The stone is thought to date from the sixth century AD and examination reveals both a fragmentary inscription in Ogham around the top, and a Latin inscription, possibly added later. Many Ogham stones were later Christianised by the addition of a cross and a Latin inscription. Ogham is a script in which the letters of the Roman alphabet are represented by short strokes. It was thought to have developed in early Christian times and was later used for writing epitaphs. Some researchers attribute the origin of the Ogham characters to the Druids.

The Island lies in Carmarthen Bay, off Giltar Point, south of Tenby.

MERLIN'S CHAIR, CARMARTHEN

Legend

Dyfed   MAP REF. SN4120

A few kilometres east of Carmarthen is Merlin's Hill,
the summit of which is said to resemble a chair. It is
from this chair that the wizard, Merlin, delivered his
prophecies. Legend has it that he is buried in the hill,
or perhaps sleeping, awaiting the call for his services
again. The sacred tree at Carmarthen is linked with
the romantic legends of Arthur. It is said that the city
will last only as long as the tree.

Carmarthen is on the A40(T), north-west of
Swansea.

Food and Drink: In Carmarthen at Ivy Bush Royal,
Spilman Street (0267 235111).

WORM'S HEAD

Legend

West Glamorgan   MAP REF. SS3887

The Worm's Head, called in Welsh Penrhyn-Gwyr, is
strangely formed, with inner and outer promontories

linked by the Devil's Bridge. To the north, a blow-hole creates a bellowing sound, which some say is the sighing of the Devil himself.

Worm's Head is approached by a signposted trackway to the south-west of Rhossili, itself at the western end of the B4247.

Food and Drink: In Rhossili at the Worms Head (0792 390512).

48. Worm's Head

49. Arthur's Stone, Cefn Bryn

ARTHUR'S STONE, CEFN BRYN

Standing stone – earthwork – burial chamber – ley – legend

Gower   MAP REF. SS5489

An ancient burial chamber, known as Maen Ceti, can be found near Reynoldston, North of Cefn Bryn. Arthur's Stone is the 25-ton capstone. Its erection has been described in ancient records as one of 'the three most arduous undertakings accomplished in Britain'. Hence the proverb: Mal gwaith Maen Cetti (Like the labour of the Stone of Cetti). It has also been described as the 'wonder of the world on Gower'. Viewing the huge stone on its supports gives much credence to this saying.

Arthur's Stone is one of the most magical stones in Wales. This is enhanced by the belief that there is an ebbing and flowing well beneath the chamber, the

128

waters of which are used for making wishes. There is a holy well about 500 metres away along Cefn Bryn, as well as a number of standing stones, all involved in a complex of ley lines. The name Arthur is probably a corruption of a more ancient word, yet it is the same Arthur who was supposed to have split the capstone with his sword. The armoured spectre which is said to emerge from beneath the stone is also believed to be that of the ancient king.

Reynoldston is signposted to the North of the A4118, to the West of Oxwich Bay. Arthur's Stone is signposted to the North of Cefn Bryn.

Food and Drink: In Reynoldston at Fairyhill Country House (0792 390139); or in Mumbles at St Annes, Western Lane (0792 369147).

PARC LE BREOS, GOWER

Burial chamber

West Glamorgan MAP REF. SS5490

This passage tomb is in an excellent state of preservation and is one of the finest to be found in Wales. Excavated in 1869 and again in 1960–1, the remains of twenty bodies were found in the various chambers along with some fragments of Neolithic pottery. The tomb is approached along a track from Parkmill. It is oval in shape, measuring approximately 18 metres by 15 metres. The passage inside is about 5 metres long with small chambers on each side.

Take the main road from Swansea, the A4118, and

turn north to Parkmill shortly before reaching Penmaen.

Food and Drink: In Mumbles at St Annes, Western Lane (0792 369147).

CARN LECHART

Stone circle – chambered tomb

West Glamorgan MAP REF. SN7006

An almost complete circle, consisting of 24 stones, can be found near the summit of Mynydd Llechart (309 metres). Inside the circle is a chambered tomb. The circle itself has a diameter of 19 metres. Carn Llechart is located near Pontardawe.

Take the A4069 north from Pontardawe towards Glenaman.

Food and Drink: In Swansea at the Beaumont, Walter Road (0792 43956); or Windsor Lodge, Mount Pleasant (0792 648996).

DYFFRYN ARDUDWY

Standing stones – earthwork – UFOs

Gwynedd MAP REF. SH5923

Two impressive cromlechs are to be found off the

A496, about seven miles north of Barmouth. They have been exposed by the removal of a massive covering cairn that would, originally, have been about 40 metres long and 17 metres wide. The two burial chambers are about 8 metres apart. As part of an outbreak of light phenomena, columns of light were seen issuing from the ground here in 1905. The site stands on the Morchras geological fault.

Take the A496 north from Barmouth to Harlech.

Food and Drink: In Barmouth at Ty'r Craig, Llanaber Road (0341 280470).

YNYSHIR STONE CIRCLE

Stone circle

Powys   MAP REF. SN9238

A typical attribute of the stone circles on the hills of Wales is that they are composed of small stones. This remote circle had 27 stones originally with a wide gap on the south-west side. Its diameter is approximately 17 metres. The Ynyshir Circle, Mynydd Eppynt, is located to the north of Sennybridge, near an artillery range.

Turn north off the A40(T) at Sennybridge, 9 miles west of Brecon, leading towards Pentre Bach.

Food and Drink: In Brecon at the Castle of Brecon, Castle Square (0874 4611); or the George, George Street (0874 3422).

THE MALWALBEE PEBBLE, LLOWES

Standing stone – legend

Powys   MAP REF. SO1941

This standing stone, no pebble as it weighs 3½ tons, is to be found in Llowes church. Called the St Meilig Cross or Malwalbee Pebble, it is said to have stood originally on a hill called Croesfeilig, from where it was transported by Malwalbee. This female ogre was supposed to have built the castle at Hay-on-Wye by magical means. The stone may have been brought down from Croesfeilig in the twelfth century, perhaps already carved with its early Christian symbols.

Llowes is on the A438, east of Hay-on-Wye.

Food and Drink: In Hay-on-Wye at Olde Black Lion, Lion Street (0497 820841); Lions Corner House, Market Street (0497 820175).

THE HOUSE OF ILLTUD (TY ILLTUD)

Burial chamber – legend – symbols

Powys   MAP REF. SO1026

The covering to this chambered cairn was removed during a nineteenth-century excavation, exposing the flat slabs that form the roof and sides. More than 60 inscribed crosses and other symbols are visible on the slabs, but they were carved at a much later date than the cairn's erection. The cairn is associated with St Illtud who is reputed to be buried at Maen Illtud, a few miles away to the west of Brecon on Mynydd Illtud, near the Brecon Beacons National Park Mountain Centre. The cairn itself is located on Manest Farm near Llanhamlach, east of Brecon.

Take the A40(T) south-east of Brecon and turn left towards Llangorse Lake.

Food and Drink: In Brecon at the George, George Street (0874 3422); or the Castle of Brecon, Castle Square (0874 4611).

TY ISAF

Burial chamber

Powys   MAP REF. SO1829

There are three chambers inside this long barrow or cairn, where the bones of 33 people were discovered when it was excavated many years ago. Found on the western side of the Black Mountains, near Pengenffordd on the A479, the cairn is over 30 metres in length and is wedge shaped. At the south end is a fourth chamber which was found to contain a Bronze Age cremation burial. There is also a false entrance, designed to confound the tomb robber, the real entrances being from the sides of the tomb.

The A479(T) runs north from the A40(T) west of Crickhowell, towards Hay-on-Wye.

Food and Drink: In Hay-on-Wye at the Olde Black Lion, Black Lion Street (0497 820841); or Lions Corner House, Market Street (0497 820175).

CRICKHOWELL

Standing stone

Powys   MAP REF. SO1820

On the bank of the river Usk is a 5.5-metre-high standing stone, the curious shape of which resembles a fish balancing upright on its tail. Local mythology describes how the stone will leap from the earth and swim in the river on Midsummer Eve. There are other standing stones in the vicinity of Crickhowell, within a short distance of the A40.

Crickhowell is on the north bank of the river Usk, on the A40. The stone is at grid reference SO183198.

Food and Drink: In Crickhowell at the Bear (0873 810408); or Glen-y-Dwr, Brecon Road (0873 810756).

GWERNVALE LONG CAIRN

Burial chamber

Powys   MAP REF. SO2119

This tomb is found beside the A40 on the west side of Crickhowell. Although no human remains were found, it is likely that they were removed during an early excavation in 1804. Excavation of the site in 1978 revealed a wedge-shaped cairn nearly 46 metres in length. Three chambers were exposed which contained various Neolithic flint implements, arrowheads and a stone axe.

The A40(T) is the main road from Abergavenny to Brecon, running alongside the River Usk at this point.

Food and Drink: In Crickhowell at the Bear (0873 810408); or Glen-y-Dwr, Brecon Road (0873 810756).

CARN BUGAIL

Burial chambers

Mid Glamorgan   MAP REF. SO1004

Found on Cefn Gelligaer, north-west of Bargoed, these two tombs, on the summit of the ridge, were once lined with large stone slabs but little is to be seen now, for they were excavated and robbed during the last century.

Turn left off the A469 which runs north from Bargoed to Tredegar, leading towards Merthyr Vale.

Food and Drink: In Blackwood at Maes Manor (0495 224551).

CATTWG'S STONE (MAEN CATTWG)

Standing stone – symbols

Mid Glamorgan   MAP REF. ST1397

Found near Gelligar, there are several cup marks to be

discovered on this stone, varying in size and depth. The squat boulder sits in a field near Heol Adam, a Roman road which leads to the Gaer camp at Brecon. The stone is named after St Cattwg, who spent some time in this vicinity during the late fifth century.

A boulder at Llanerch Farm in Powys had 31 cups carved on it in four rows. The largest number discovered on a single stone in Wales is on a burial chamber near Clynnog Fawr, in Gwynedd, where the capstone displays 110 cup markings.

Take the A472 north from Caerphilly, and turn right onto the B4254 towards Gelligar at Nelson.

Food and Drink: In Caerphilly at Griffin Inn Motel, Rudry (0222 869735).

TWYN TUDOR

Earthwork – burial mound – legend

Gwent   MAP REF. ST1994

Located at Mynyddislwyn, this mysterious mound may be the monumental grave mound of an early British king. There are various legends associated with it however, and one recalls how a Roman army was overwhelmed by a vast horde of Celts, the slaughtered soldiers being buried beneath the huge mound.

Twyn Tudor is to be found south of Pontllanfriats on the A4048 leading towards Newport.

Food and Drink: In Newport at Westgate, Commercial Street (0633 244444).

TWM BARLWM

Earthwork – burial mound – legend

Gwent   MAP REF. ST2493

Known locally as 'the pimple', there is an impressive mound on the summit of Risca. According to local legend, an important Celtic chief is buried inside the mound. It is possible that it was constructed as a monumental tomb but then later converted by the Normans into a motte.

Take the A467 north from Newport towards Ebbw Vale and the hill is on the right above Crosskeys.

Food and Drink: In Newport at Westgate, Commercial Street (0633 244444).

LLANFIHANGEL ROGIET

Standing stone – ley

Gwent   MAP REF. ST4587

The Devil's Quoit is a standing stone in a field to the west of Llanfihangel Rogiet church. Local folklore explains how the stone was hurled by the Devil from Portishead when he was in a fit of temper. The stone is on a ley alignment which connects the fort on Wilcrick Hill with the stone, with Rogiet church, Portskewett church and Black Rock, to the west of Charston Rock.

Llanfihangel Rogiet is signposted to the west of

Caldicott, itself best approached from junction 22 of the M4.

Food and Drink: In Chepstow at the Beaufort, Beaufort Square, St Mary Street (02912 2497); or Castle View, Bridge Street (02912 70349).

SUDBROOK

Church – holy well

Gwent   MAP REF. ST5288

The chapel of St Tecia is now ruinous, but it was in use in the thirteenth century. St Tecia was once St Triads and occultists suggest that the name derived from the Roman word *theriac*, which was a sort of syrup made by magical means from the flesh of vipers. The chapel was once on land that was joined to the mainland and was built to service a holy well, the remains of which may still be seen. The chapel remains may be safely visited at low tide.

Sudbrook is located south-east of Caldicot, approached from junction 23 of the M4.

Food and Drink: In Chepstow at the Beaufort, Beaufort Square, St Mary Street (02912 2497); or Castle View, Bridge Street (02912 70349).

THE HAROLD'S STONES, TRELLECK

Standing stones – legend

Gwent   MAP REF. SO5005

According to legend, the three stones standing in a field on the outskirts of Trelleck, were thrown there by a giant from the summit of Ysgyryd Fawr. Although the three stones have been erected in a straight line, they lean in different directions.

Trelleck is on the B4293 minor road which runs north from Chepstow to Monmouth.

Food and Drink: In Whitebrook at the Crown at Whitebrook (0600 860254).

50. Harold's Stones, Trelleck

SOUTH AND EAST

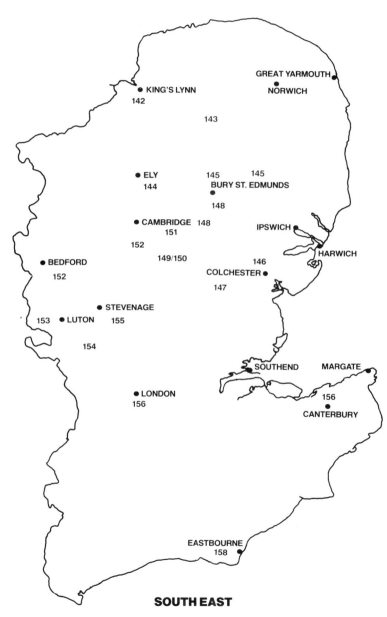

GREAT YARMOUTH

KING'S LYNN
142

NORWICH

143

ELY
144

145

145
BURY ST. EDMUNDS

148

CAMBRIDGE 148
151

IPSWICH

152

149/150

HARWICH

BEDFORD
152

146

COLCHESTER

147

STEVENAGE

153 LUTON 155

154

SOUTHEND

MARGATE

156

CANTERBURY

LONDON
156

EASTBOURNE
158

SOUTH EAST

SOUTH

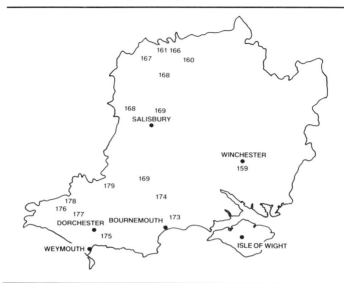

TUESDAY MARKET STREET, KING'S LYNN

Witchcraft – magic

Norfolk   MAP REF. TF6119

Above one of the windows of number 15, Tuesday Market Street, there is the image of a heart contained within a diamond shape. In June 1616, the wife of a glovemaker was hanged as a witch in Tuesday Market Square, which then contained the market cross, and was used for such public executions. The woman died protesting her innocence and shortly before she was hanged she predicted that when she expired her heart would fly out from her body and perch on the window of the magistrate who had condemned her.

King's Lynn is on the junction of the A17(T) and the A10.

Food and Drink: In King's Lynn at Stuart House, Goodwins Road (0553 772169); or Tudor Rose, 11 St Nicholas Street, off Tuesday Market Place (0553 762824).

SWAFFHAM CHURCH

Church – hermeticism – symbols

Norfolk   MAP REF. TF8109

The esoteric symbolism found in the church's wooden ceiling includes exquisitely wrought angels, poppyheads, including the mythical 'pedlar' of Swaffham, the pedlar's dog, the four evangelist symbols and two beautiful pelicans feeding their young with blood, an arcane symbol for the Christ. The rosary on two of the poppyheads is arranged with the arms of those who hold them to form a figure eight, the lemniscate. The figure is constructed to represent, at its mystic centre, the point where man and God meet.

Swaffham is situated south of the junction of the A47(T) and the A1065.

Food and Drink: In Swaffham at the George, Station Road (0760 21238).

ELY CATHEDRAL

Cathedral – hermeticism – symbols

Cambridgeshire   MAP REF. TL5380

To be found in this cathedral are many occult and hermetic symbols. For example, there are symbols of the stars and the sun and moon, orientated so that the crescent of the moon points away from the sun. This, derived from alchemical symbolism, portrays the male and female power energies in the created world, in a state of tension. The resolution is to be found in the Healer Christ. The sun represents the masculine energies of intellect and the spirit, the moon represents the feminine attributes of feeling and the heart. In alchemy, their holy marriage as uniting King and Queen, results in the birth of a divine child, or alchemical 'gold'.

Noteable also is the geometric maze which is set in the floor tiles immediately below the west tower. Note well also the demonic scenes depicted among the misericords of the choir stalls. In one, the devil leads two clerics, as though they were old friends.

Ely is signposted off the A10(T) at the junction with the A142.

Food and Drink: In Ely at Fenlands Lodge, Soham Road, Stutney – 3 kilometres south-east on the A142 – (0353 67047); or Old Fire Engine House, 25 St Mary's Street (0353 2582).

MOYSE'S HALL MUSEUM

Witchcraft – magic

Suffolk   MAP REF. TL8564

In Bury St Edmunds, the pride of the witchcraft paraphernalia in the Moyse's Hall Museum is a genuine witch poppet, a doll made by witches used in the ritualistic casting of spells. The collection includes witch-bottles, and numerous charms against witchcraft.

Bury St Edmunds is on the A45(T) junction with the A143. The museum is in the Cornhill.

Food and Drink: In Bury St Edmunds at the Angel, Angel Hill (0284 753926); or Ravenwood Hall, Rougham – 5 kilometres east off the A45 – (0359 70345).

ST JOHN'S, ELMSWELL

Church – symbols

Suffolk   MAP REF. TL9863

The stone symbols on the church tower and south façade of St John the Baptist in Elmswell have been described as a 'numerologist's paradise'. The designs include every significant astrological grade from one to forty, plus many esoteric symbols, such as the pentagram, chalices and the vased lily (refer to St John's Gateway, Colchester).

Elmswell is situated north-east of Woolpit at the junction of the A45(T) and the A1088.

Food and Drink: In Bury St Edmunds at the Angel, Angel Hill (0284 753926); or Ravenwood Hall, Rougham – 5 kilometres east off the A45 – (0359 70345).

ST JOHN'S GATEWAY, COLCHESTER

Hermeticism – symbols

Essex   MAP REF. TM0025

Stonework vases and lilies on the façade of St John's Gateway to the old priory are interesting survivals of hermetic symbols. The lily is derived from an occult symbolism which holds that when the Milky Way of stars was made in the skies, so the lily was made on earth. The belief is that what is enacted in the heavens must be reflected on the earth: the stars were made at the same time as the spirit of man descended to live on the earth plane. This accounts for the lily's appearance on a building linked with St John, whose Gospel deals with the incarnation of the Logos or Word, into the earth plane.

Colchester is east of the A12(T) at the roundabout junction with the A604.

Food and Drink: In Colchester at the George, 116 High Street (0206 578494); or Kings Ford Park, Layer Road, Layer de la Haye – 4 kilometres south on the B1026 – (0206 34301).

PAYCOCK HOUSE, COGGESHALL

Occult centre – symbols

Essex   MAP REF. TL8523

The façade of Paycock House displays a long wooden frieze, depicting the story of progress from the demonic levels that beset man to the spiritual clarity and awareness that come with initiation. The left of the frieze begins with the image of a dragon, representing the demonic, while the frieze concludes with the image of a man wearing a phrygian cap, one of the common mediaeval symbols of initiation. The cap is similar to the one found in many images of the Mithraic cult, popular among the invading legions of Rome.

Coggeshall is situated west of the junction of the A120 and A12(T).

Food and Drink: In Colchester at the George, 116 High Street (0206 578494); or Kings Ford Park, Layer Road, Layer de la Haye – 4 kilometres south on the B1026 – (0206 34301).

BORLEY RECTORY

Haunting – legend

Suffolk   MAP REF. TL8442

The psychic investigator, Harry Price, made famous the hauntings of Borley Rectory. Despite Price being exposed as a charlatan and liar, it is still popularly believed that the Rectory is haunted, and that in 1939 it was burned down by some supernatural phenomenon. The nearby church of Borley seems to be genuinely haunted by a variety of ghosts, from a spirit nun to a phantom coach, so that Price may have missed his real chance to confront the paranormal.

Borley is signposted off the B1064, north-west of Sudbury.

Food and Drink: In Sudbury at the Ballingdon Grove, Middleton Road (0787 75781).

SIBLE HEDINGHAM

Witchcraft – magic

Essex   MAP REF. TL7834

Visit the Swan Inn in this village where one of the last fatal witch swimmings took place. On 3 August 1865, an old Frenchman who had a reputation as a warlock, and who made his living telling fortunes (in spite of being deaf and dumb) was attacked by one Emma Smith of Ridgwell. A crowd gathered and dragged the

148

unfortunate man down to the river by the side of what is now Aberford Street, down to Rawlinson's Mill, and pushed him in to swim as a witch. The next day the man died of exposure, and although Emma Smith continued to insist that she had been bewitched by the old man, she and an accomplice were tried for murder.

Sible Hedingham is at the junction of the A604 and B1058.

Food and Drink: In Sudbury at Ballingdon Grove, Middleton Road (0787 75781).

TURF MAZE, SAFFRON WALDEN

Earthwork – power point – rituals

Essex   MAP REF. TL5338

The largest turf-cut maze in England is to be found at Saffron Walden, to the eastern side of the common. The date of its original construction is unknown, but records show that in 1699 payment was made for redefining its extent and re-cutting its formal pattern. In 1911, the chalk underbase was laid with red bricks in an attempt to preserve it. At one time there were numerous turf-cut mazes in Britain, but now few remain. It has been suggested that mazes were originally astronomical observatories. Harold Bayley has said that, 'It would seem highly probable that the knot, maze, Troy Town, or trou town, primarily was emblematic of the Maze or Womb of Life, conceived either physically or etherically in accord with the spirit of the time and people.' Mazes are frequently called Troy Town or The Walls of Troy, and Troy Towns or Draytons appear in many parts of the country.

Spirals carved on the stones of Newgrange in Ireland may also represent the Maze of Life, echoing the idea that burial inside elaborate burial mounds symbolised a return to the womb. Inside St Mary's church is a beautifully coloured tapestry kneeler, depicting the Saffron Walden maze.

Saffron Walden is signposted to the east of the B1383, off junction 9 of the M11.

Food and Drink: In Saffron Walden at the Saffron, 10-18 High Street (0799 22676); or Old Hoops, 15 King Street (0799 22813).

WANDLEBURY CHALK FIGURE

Hill figure – legend

Cambridgeshire   MAP REF. TL4953

The three huge chalk figures on Wandlebury Hill have been linked with the Gog-Magog legends. The discoverer, T.C. Lethbridge, described the figure as a goggle-eyed goddess with chariot and horses. Later interpreters see it as a god (or goddess) with a dragon. Names similar to Gog and Magog were respectively lunar and solar gods of the British Iron Age. Some associate Gog with the Celtic god, Ogma, who is reputed to have constructed the magical Ogham lapidary alphabet. The details of Lethbridge's search and a fuller interpretation of his findings are recorded in his book, *Gogmagog: The Buried Gods.*

Gog Magog Hills is north of the A1307, south-east of Cambridge. The figures are, however, covered over now.

Food and Drink: In Cambridge at Arundel House, Chesterton Road (0223 67701); or Midsummer House, Midsummer Common (0223 69299).

ROYSTON CAVE

Witchcraft – magic – rituals – symbols

Hertfordshire   MAP REF. TL3541

In Royston is a unique cave, about 9 metres below ground, the walls of which are covered in extraordinary glyphs of unknown origin or purpose. One or two of the symbols are distinctly occult, and appear to be involved with the darker side of magic.

Royston is on the A10(T), south-west of Cambridge. The tunnel's entrance is in Baldock Street.

Food and Drink: In Cambridge at Arundel House, 53 Chesterton Road (0223 67701); or Midsummer House, Midsummer Common (0223 69299).

CASTLE HILL

Earthwork – ley

Bedfordshire   MAP REF. TL1037

Found near Clophill, this earthwork is marked on the map as 'Castle Hill'. You will find a typical example of the banks and ditches surrounding a central mound through which leys often pass. 'In cases where the earthwork covers a large area, and consists of banks and ditches surrounding a huge flat expanse, any leys passing through the site usually only touch one of the encircling banks rather than passing right through the centre of the site. This is because later earthworks often incorporated earlier mounds or tumuli in their banks, and it is through these early constructions that the leys pass' (*Mysterious Britain,* Janet and Colin Bord).

Clophill is on the A6(T) south of Bedford and the hill is reached by taking the A507 to Baldock.

Food and Drink: In Bedford at De Parys, De Parys Avenue (0234 52121); or the Bedford Swan, The Embankment (0234 46565).

DUNSTABLE DOWNS

Earthwork

Bedfordshire   MAP REF. TL0121

High up on the Dunstable Downs, at a place called Five Knolls, can be found burial mounds that date from 1500 BC. Excavation has revealed the burials that took place there. A visit to this place is worth it just for the view but you will also experience the mystical atmosphere that pervades this ancient burial ground.

The Downs are in the south-east of Dunstable, which is at junction 11 of the M1, west of Luton.

Food and Drink: In Dunstable at the Highwayman, London Road (0582 601122).

DEVIL'S DYKE, WHEATHAMPSTEAD

Earthwork

Hertfordshire   MAP REF. TL1814

This earthwork is thought to be the site of Julius Caesar's attack in 54 BC on the tribal headquarters of Cassivellaunus. If so, once the scene of terrible violence, all now lies peaceful under an arch of protective trees. Devil's Dyke is about 12 metres deep and 27 metres wide, with steep banks on either side. Another dyke, called the Slad, lies a little to the east and together they are thought to have comprised one earthwork, covering approximately 100 acres.

Wheathampstead is west of Welwyn Garden City on the B653 to Luton.

Food and Drink: In Harpenden at Glen Eagles, Luton Road (05827 60271).

KNEBWORTH HOUSE

Alchemy – hermeticism

Hertfordshire MAP REF. TL2420

Birthplace and home of Sir Edward Bulwer Lytton, famous amongst occultists for his book on Rosicrucianism, *Zanoni*, his life of the alchemist physician, Paracelsus, Knebworth House was the family seat of the Lytton family. Sir Edward introduced the word 'vril' into occult lore, about which Madame Blavatsky wrote, 'The name vril may be a fiction; the Force itself is a fact . . . mentioned in all the secret works [and could] reduce Europe in a few days to its primitive chaotic state with no man left alive to tell the tale.' Blavatsky wrote these words in 1888, long before man had tampered with atomic forces.

Knebworth House is in Old Knebworth, to the west of Knebworth, which is signposted to the west of the A602, south of Stevenage.

Food and Drink: In Stevenage at the Roebuck, Old London Road, Broadwater (0438 365444); or Stevenage Moat House, High Street, Old Town – Queens Moat (0438 359111).

BRITISH MUSEUM

Ghosts – legends – astrology – magic – symbols

London   MAP REF. TQ2981

There are few important works by occultists and esotericists that are not represented in the finest collection of occult books in the world, housed in the British Library and the related manuscript departments of the British Museum. In the museum's collection of occult items, those on display include the sixteenth-century scrying glass used by the magician, Dr John Dee. The museum now also contains artefacts from the famous occult collection of the Wellbeing Institute, moved from the Institute's library on Marylebone Road. Items include books which are said to have been bound with human skin.

The British Museum is in Bloomsbury and the nearest tube station is Tottenham Court Road.

Food and Drink: In Bloomsbury at the Hotel Russell, Russell Square (071-837 6470); or Winston's Eating House, 24 Coptic Street (071-580 3422).

CANTERBURY CATHEDRAL

Cathedral – astrology – symbols

Kent   MAP REF. TR1557

A beautiful marble inlay decorates the floor of Trinity

Chapel in the cathedral, and depicts twelve pictures of the zodiacal signs, the corresponding 'monthly labours' and what were probably the corresponding 'virtues and vices' of the zodiac. Although most are almost worn away, one or two of the distinctive designs are clearly visible. The one associated with Libra, for example, is an ancient symbol for what modern occultists call the 'etheric', the vital life-force of the cosmos. Pilgrims who may wish to learn more of the background to the 12 labours and the associated astrological symbolism, should obtain a copy of *The Labours of Hercules* by Alice A. Bailey and published by the Lucis Press – a true esoteric document.

Also in Trinity Chapel is the effigy-tomb to Edward, the Black Prince. His father, Edward III, was said to be held captive by the necromancy of his mistress, Alice Perrers.

Canterbury is signposted from the A2, between Faversham and Dover.

Food and Drink: In Canterbury at the Canterbury, 71 New Dover Road (0227 450551); or Waterfield's, 5 Best Lane (0227 450276).

THE LONG MAN OF WILMINGTON

Hill figure – power point

East Sussex   MAP REF. TQ5405

This hill figure, featureless and holding a staff in each hand, is cut on the downland grass on Windover Hill, and is probably 2000 years old. Some occultists suggest that it is an image of the pagan god, Helith. The Long Man was restored in the late nineteenth century in such a way that it is difficult to see exactly what it looked like when first devised. It is thought by some that the figure may have been emasculated during renovation. He was known as the Green Man before this deed. The figure is over 70 metres tall and, like most hill figures was seemingly designed to be viewed to best advantage from the air! He has been thought to represent many characters, Beowulf, Woden, Thor, Apollo and Mercury among them, but to ley hunters he is the prehistoric surveyor, holding his sighting staffs. The late T.C. Lethbridge recalled being told by a shepherd that the Long Man once had a companion, and that the two figures were known as Adam and Eve.

The Long Man is south-east of the village, signposted towards Westdean, between the A27 and A259.

Food and Drink: In Lewes at the White Hart, High Street (0273 474676).

THE ROUND TABLE, WINCHESTER

Legend

Hampshire   MAP REF. SU4729

In the Great Hall of Winchester castle can be found a representation of King Arthur's original Round Table. The circle is divided into 25 painted segments, alternating in yellows and greens. The central floral design is made from two superimposed roses, one red, one white, which suggests that the panel was painted in the fifteenth century, perhaps for a masque connected with the Arthurian stories.

While in Winchester, visit the ancient fort system, of which St Catherine's Hill is a part. The top of the hill sports a turf maze of distinctive pattern and unknown age.

Winchester is immediately west of the M3, junction 10.

Food and Drink: In Winchester at the Royal, St Peter Street (0962 53468); or Lockes, 1st Floor, 5 Jewry Street (0962 60007).

MERLIN'S MOUNT

Earthwork – hill figure – power point

Wiltshire   MAP REF. SU1869

Standing today within the grounds of Marlborough College is the terraced form of Merlin's Mount, a similar earthwork to that described under Tynwald Hill on the Isle of Man, which is still in use. Merlin's Mount is situated about 8 kilometres east of Avebury. On its top is cut the crude outline of a white horse, probably cut in 1804 by the scholars of a local educational establishment.

Marlborough is on the A4 between Hungerford and Avebury, 11 kilometres south of junction 15 of the M4.

Food and Drink: In Marlborough at Merlin, High Street (0672 52151); or Ivy House, High Street (0672 515333).

51. Merlin's Mount. The inner walls of the grotto at its foot are lined with sea shells

AVEBURY

Stone circles – standing stones – earthwork – rituals

Wiltshire   MAP REF. SU0969

Perhaps the most important ancient site in the British Isles, the Avebury site consists of a huge complex of stone circles, earthworks and avenues over 1280 metres in circumference. The stone circles and avenues were first erected as a Sun Temple some 5000 years ago. It is said that priests would charge the standing stones with a guardian spirit, or earth being. The variety of surrounding sites, Silbury Hill, the Kennet Avenue, Windmill Hill and the West Kennet Long Barrow, as well as numerous processional ways, mark this as one of the most important religious or ceremonial centres of the ancient western world.

About a mile from Avebury, on the Chippenham to Marlborough road is Silbury Hill, the largest prehistoric earthwork in Europe. It has been calculated that gangs of up to 700 men would have taken ten years to pack the materials from which it is constructed. The earliest part of the mound is dated approximately 2000 BC. A shaft dug into the mound in 1967–70 showed that it was constructed on similar principles of inner-platform construction as was used in the pyramid-building of ancient Egypt.

Surrounding the whole area of the Avebury complex is a great earth bank, and within this is the outer circle of stones, weighing up to 40 tons. Originally, there were 100, but the number is reduced today to 27.

52. *Avebury*

53. *The Cove*

54. *Silbury Hill*

55. *Silbury Hill from the Sanctuary*

Within this circle of stones there are remnants of two smaller ones, each originally of about 30 stones.

The ruins of this great sun temple are in the care of the Department of the Environment. Despite the awesome impression that the experience of Avebury leaves upon the observer, little of the original grandeur remains. Most of the stones were smashed up in the seventeenth and eighteenth centuries, and have been used to build the village houses and local farms.

Considering now one of the main avenues of standing stones, the Kennet Avenue, there were originally 200 stones along its route. Far fewer remain today, but those that do clearly demonstrate that they were erected in a fashion that alternates between wide, angular-shaped stones, and thinner, straighter ones.

Scattered around the surrounding landscape are other major monuments, some even older than the henge. We have mentioned Silbury Hill. To the north-west of the henge is Windmill Hill, a natural feature of the landscape that was earthworked in early Neolithic times. This was some kind of gathering place for hundreds of years prior to the construction of the Avebury henge. To the south-east is the Sanctuary, a circular site built from stones and posts at the end of the Kennet Avenue. It is marked now only by concrete plinths. Elsewhere in the landscape are great long barrows, pre-dating the henge. Scattered amongst all these are later Bronze Age round barrows and the locations of lost sites.

Paul Devereux describes in *Earth Memory* how many visits to Avebury helped him to develop, 'the distinct sense that Silbury Hill was communicating in some way. I slowly began to think of it as a teacher – a living, sentient teacher. Such an animistic idea would of

56. *Avebury village*

course make any archaeologist, any Western rationalist, wail in despair. I felt uneasy about it myself to begin with, but soon learned to adopt the attitude with ease.'

The message in this is clear to all who visit such sacred sites. It is we who are the pupils and it is the mysteries of the earth at such places as Silbury that have so much to teach us, despite our often misplaced superior attitude to the knowledge once held by the ancient world.

Avebury is on the A4361, south of Swindon.

Food and Drink: In Marlborough at Merlin, High Street (0672 521151).

AVEBURY CHURCH

Church – symbols

Wiltshire   MAP REF. SU1070

The carving on the twelfth-century font in Avebury church is an obvious reference to the battle between the serpent power worship of the pre-Christian temple at Avebury, and the new Christianity. The carved image depicts a winged serpent biting the foot of a bishop. He in turn is striking the serpent with his staff or crozier. Avebury was one of the more resistant centres to the new teachings of Christianity. The serpent has now become synonymous with the Devil.

Avebury lies on the A4, 11 kilometres west of Marlborough and 11 kilometres north of Devizes.

Food and Drink: In Devizes at the Bear Hotel, The Market Place (0380 722444).

57. Carvings on the font of St James church, Avebury

58. Cherhill White Horse

THE CHERHILL WHITE HORSE

Hill figure

Wiltshire   MAP REF. SU0370

Supposedly cut in 1780 by a Dr Alsop, this figure is probably a new cutting, based on the much more ancient one still to be found at Uffington in central England.

To find this hill figure, take the A4 between Calne and Cherhill. The best view can be obtained from the hills to the north of Cherhill. Look out for the tall obelisk monument and the sign for Oldbury Castle. Between the White Horse and the monument lies Oldbury Camp, an earthwork built 2,000 years ago.

Food and Drink: In Marlborough at Merlin, High Street (0672 52151).

WANSDYKE

Earthwork

Wiltshire　MAP REF. SU1365

Wansdyke, near Marlborough, is a great dyke that stretches across the southern edge of the Avebury/ Silbury Hill complex, and as such could have some connection with that important occult centre. The ramparts stretch across Somerset and Wiltshire, although it is not continuous. Possibly built in the sixth century AD as a defensive frontier, the name Wansdyke derives from that of the Anglo-Saxon god, Woden, *Wodens dic*, who was an important deity to the early English.

Leave Marlborough by the A345 south and then west on minor roads to Devizes, travelling along the Vale of Pewzey.

Food and Drink: In Marlborough at Ivy House, High Street (0672 515333); or Merlin, High Street (0672 52151).

WARMINSTER

Power point – leys

Wiltshire　MAP REF. ST8744

The town of Warminster lies on the intersection of over a dozen important ley lines and is well known for the UFO activity which takes place over this proclaimed power point, or centre for esoteric earth energies. Wiltshire is an area of the country also now becoming known for the inexplicable appearance of crop circles, flattened areas of corn that are completely symmetrical in nature and which appear to be made not by human hand. The corn bends but does not break and therefore continues to grow. The circles can spring up overnight.

Cley Hill is the centre for crop circles. This is a prehistoric, earthworked natural hill. In the 1960s, during the height of the UFO reportings, balls of light were seen to issue from the ground, and also shoot down into it. Cley Hill stands on one of the very few surface geological faults in the region (the Warminster fault).

Warminster is on the A350, north of Shaftesbury.

Food and Drink: In Warminster at the Old Bell, Market Place (0985 216611).

STONEHENGE

Stone circle – standing stones – leys – ritual

Wiltshire   MAP REF. SU1343

A simple observation that reveals the startling complexity of thought, design and ingenuity that went into the construction of this most well-known of sacred sites, is that the surviving lintels, fitted originally end-to-end on tongue and groove joints, all dressed on a curve, were designed to allow the eye to adjust for the

59. *A view of Stonehenge from Stone 91, one of the four 'Station Stones', positions which form a rectangle that gives all the important solar and lunar sightlines*

60. *Looking along the midsummer sunrise axis of Stonehenge towards the outlying Heel Stone. The shorter stones are the famous Stonehenge bluestones. The big stones and lintels are the later sarsen stones*

61. *View of Stonehenge from the northwest*

62. *View through the uprights of one of the inner trilithons to a gap in the outer sarsen circle. Gerald Hawkins calculated that this method of sighting framed sections of the skyline where important sun or moon rises/sets occurred*

natural foreshortening of perspective. Those researchers who do not adopt a prosaic stance see Stonehenge as the last truly great link with a long-lost past, when magic structures were built to coordinate ceremonials and ritual with the energies of the universe – the purpose of initiation.

Charles Walker explains how Stonehenge was called *chior-gaur* in ancient times, meaning approximately dance of giants, reminding us that even by the twelfth century the chronicler Geoffrey of Monmouth still called the circle the Giant's Dance, though he knew as little of the meaning or purpose of the stones as we do today. The huge blocks high above their heads caused the Saxons to name the structure 'hanging stones', from which the present 'Stonehenge' is thought to be derived.

Professor G.S. Hawkins has recently used a computer to examine the immense number of alignments that the sun and moon, rising and setting at different times of the year, make with the stones and spaces between the trilithons. He has found that Stonehenge can be used as an accurate predictor of the movements of the heavenly bodies and to predict eclipses.

It is certain that the 60 bluestones, which form a double circle as part of the structure, were not natural to this locality. Wherever their source, the question remains, why did the builders want these particular stones? The bluestones, brought from the Preseli Mountains in South Wales or perhaps even further afield, are not particularly decorative. They have a bluish tint only when freshly fractured, and this soon fades with weathering – *and* there were plenty of good, big stones in the locality, some of which were indeed used.

Geoffrey of Monmouth relates how Merlin the magician by his secret art moved stones from Ireland to 'the mount of Ambrius', which has been identified as Amesbury, very near Stonehenge, and earlier the stones were brought from Africa to Ireland by 'giants who were magicians'.

In our materialistic age it is too easy to dismiss such legends. It is a way of appreciating their worth to consider not their truth but the *effect* that they had on those that propagated them. The power of a belief is not held in its correctness or otherwise, but in its holding. Certainly the powers at work during the conception and building of Stonehenge, well over 4000 years ago, were as great as any that we know of today.

Stonehenge can be seen to the north of the A303, to the west of the junction with the A360.

Food and Drink: In Salisbury at the Red Lion, Milford Street (0722 23334); or the Cathedral, Milford Street (0722 20144).

CHRISTCHURCH

Church – legends – symbols

Dorset   MAP REF. SZ1592

A mysterious carpenter who worked on the site when the priory church at Christchurch was built is said to have been Christ himself. Several other myths are now attached to the building of this church. In Christian symbolism, the Christ is associated with fish and the zodiacal sign for Pisces, the sign of the fish. In the church's nave is a tombstone, dated 1688, which incorporates the sigil for Pisces in its inscription. In astrological lore, the Age of Pisces preceded the Age of Aquarius, into which we are now entering, so perhaps if such images were carved today it would be the picture of the Water Bearer, rather than the Fish, which would take precedence.

The church is to the south of the town, which is signposted south of the A337.

Food and Drink: In Christchurch at the Fisherman's Haunt, Salisbury Road, Winkton – 4 kilometres north on the B3347 – (0202 477283); or Splinters, 12 Church Street (0202 483454).

BADBURY RINGS

Earthwork – occult centre

Dorset   MAP REF. ST9603

Badbury Rings, near Wimborne Minster, is one of the most spectacular earthworks in the county of Dorset. Attributed to the Iron Age, the site has never been excavated, and may be much older. Roman roads meet here and it was once the site of an ancient moot, where the local chieftains would meet to discuss 'political' matters. Three outer banks wind round the pine-topped hill, reminiscent of the ritual mazes thought to be part of pagan rituals. Two entrances to the site face east and west, indicating that the site's prime purpose was probably not defensive but for religious, ritual activities.

Travelling north-west from Bournemouth, the earthworks are on the right-hand side of the B3082 between Wimborne Minster and Blandford Forum.

Food and Drink: In Blandford Forum at the Crown, West Street (0258 56626).

MAIDEN CASTLE

Earthwork – temple – occult centre

Dorset   MAP REF. SY6788

This is a huge prehistoric earthwork near Dorchester covering an area of 120 acres, with an average width of 460 metres and length of 900 metres. It is impractical to think that this 'hillfort' was originally conceived as a defensive position – it has been estimated that 250,000 men would have been required to defend it. Many of these hillforts have two entrances, one north of east and the other south of west, suggesting some form of ceremonial related to the sun. The labyrinthine east and west entrances may have been built as a way for processional entry by people of the Neolithic era. After AD 367, the Romans built a temple within the enclosure, whose remains are still clearly visible.

The site is approached on the A354 running south from Dorchester, to the west of the road.

Food and Drink: In Dorchester at the King's Arms (0305 65353).

63. Maiden Castle, Dorset

TOLLER FRATRUM

Hermeticism – church – rituals

Dorset   MAP REF. SY5797

In Toller Fratrum, the House of Toller may have been used by the Knights Hospitallers (the Knights of St John of Jerusalem), an esoteric movement which introduced new methods of healing into Europe from the East.

The small church of St Basil, behind what used to be the refectory, has a stone carving depicting Mary Magdalene washing Christ's feet. In washing His feet – the feet are ruled by Pisces – with the hair of her head – the head is ruled by Aries – the image depicts that the Age of Aries had given way to that of Pisces.

176

Toller Fratrum is south of the A356, north-west of Dorchester.

Food and Drink: In Dorchester at the King's Arms (0305 65353).

THE CERNE ABBAS GIANT

Hill figure – earthwork

Dorset   MAP REF. ST6601

Cut into the slope of the downs, approximately half a kilometre from the village of Cerne Abbas is a huge outline figure, wielding a club and sporting a huge phallus. The figure is 54.8 metres high and the phallus is 9.1 metres long. The outline of the figure is a 60-cm deep trench filled with chalk. The giant may be an idol of the pagan god, Helith, and is associated with rites of fertility. Found high behind the giant is a terraced earthwork, the Trendle, or The Frying Pan, which also is said to have been sacred ground associated with a fertility cult, and was the probable site of Maypole dancing. It is said that walking seven times around the giant's phallus will ensure fertility, a practice which, I am assured, persists today.

The village lies on the A352, to the north of Dorchester, with the giant to the east of the road.

Food and Drink: In Dorchester at the King's Arms (0305 65353).

64. Cerne Abbas Giant

ST PETER'S, CHETNOLE

Church – symbols

Dorset   MAP REF. ST6007

Four demonic creatures adorn the sixteenth-century tower of the church of St Peter in the village of Chetnole. This church sports some of the most interesting gargoyles in England, for travellers fascinated by the grotesque.

Chetnole is located south of Yeovil, to the east of the A37.

Food and Drink: In Yeovil at the Preston, 64 Preston Road (0935 74400); or Little Barwick House, Barwick Village – 3 kilometres south of the A37 (0935 23902).

SANDFORD ORCAS

Ghost – haunting

Dorset   MAP REF. ST6220

If you are in search of a haunted house, then you could do worse than the manor house of this village with its retinue of fourteen ghosts. These include the spirit of a pet dog, a phantom spinet-player, a 'Lady in Green', a 'Lady in Red', an Elizabethan lady, the spirit of a man who committed suicide in the gatehouse and the ghost of a previous owner, Sir Hubert Medlycott. There are probably more!

Sandford Orcas is signposted east of the B3148, north-east of Yeovil.

Food and Drink: In Sherborne at Eastbury, Long Street (0935 813131); or The Post House, Horsecastles Lane (0935 813191).

SOUTH-WEST

SOUTH WEST EXCLUDING CORNWALL

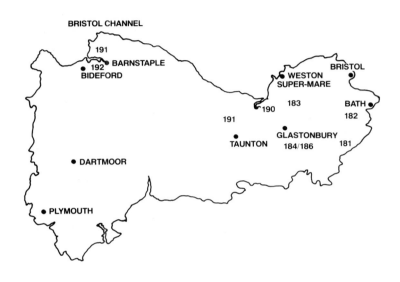

CORNWALL

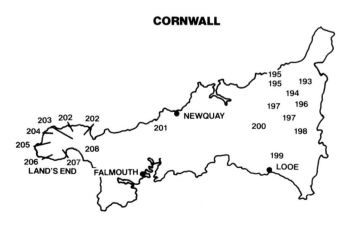

BREWHAM FOREST

Witchcraft – magic

Somerset   MAP REF. ST7236

There is a revival today of interest in Wicca, the nature religions, and practices that purport to control and manipulate natural powers and energies. Much prejudice against this movement, which often simply wishes to emphasise our connection with and responsibility for the natural world, stems from the practices of witches and warlocks in centuries passed. The seventeenth-century historian, Joseph Glanvill, refers to the witch sabbats held in the forest here. Those attending were proficient in making wax amulets, used for evil purposes. Those attending these sabbats, included Julian Cox, who was hanged as a warlock at Taunton, in 1664. On visiting this place and sensing the atmosphere, it is interesting to intuit whether the remaining atmosphere indicates the evil deeds that were purported to have taken place.

Brewham Forest is north-east of Brewham, signposted off the A359, north of Bruton.

Food and Drink: In Bruton at Truffles, 95 High Street (0749 812255).

ABBEY CHURCH, BATH

Church – alchemy – hermeticism

Avon   MAP REF. ST7464

After the dissolution of the abbey in 1539, Prior Holeway continued to live in the Priory House in front of the abbey. He gathered an important school of alchemical research, including the alchemist Thomas Charnock. The exoteric face of alchemy was the common understanding of it as a search for the substance which would turn base metals into gold. From this search has developed our modern science of chemistry. From this point of view alone, alchemy is of interest. But more than this, the esoteric alchemy was a psychological and spiritual process, a search for inner gold, symbol of the Son of God. The alchemical view is that He is to be found *in* the world, in fact in us, and not in a distant heaven. Many of the symbols to be found

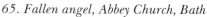

65. Fallen angel, Abbey Church, Bath

around the abbey are alchemical in origin, such as the carving on the west front, which depicts the ladders to heaven. Climbed by angels, one of them falls to become a devil. During the First World War, the image of a soldier's face developed on a wall in the abbey. It attracted such crowds that the authorities took steps to remove the image.

The abbey church is in central Bath, west of the River Avon.

Food and Drink: Duke's, Great Pulteney Street (0225 63512); or The Compass Hotel, North Parade (0225 461603).

STANTON DREW

Stone circle – standing stones – legend

Somerset　MAP REF. ST6063

Here again, as described under the heading of 'The Blind Fiddler', we meet with the idea that standing stones are associated with a musician – this time that awesome fiddler, the Devil himself. At this stone circle we also encounter the idea that the stones were once people who now repent at leisure for their sins. The stones at Stanton Drew, three stone circles, two stone avenues, the Cove and a fallen standing stone, Hautville's Quoit, are said to be Saturday-night revellers at a wedding celebration. The visiting musician, a fiddler, made the guests dance faster and faster. They could not stop – until dawn when it became clear that the fiddler was the Devil. He said that one day he would

66. Stanton Drew

return and play to them again. Until that day comes, they remain as stones in the field at Stanton Drew.

Stanton Drew is south of the B3130, east of Chew Magna.

Food and Drink: In Bath at Duke's, Gt Pulteney Street (0225 63512); or Menage à Deux, 2 George Street (0225 63341).

CHALICE WELL, GLASTONBURY

Power point – holy well

Somerset   MAP REF. ST5139

Visit the gardens at Chalice Well on Chalice Hill next

to the Tor, and you will discover the famous well lid, wrought in iron in the shape of the *vesica piscis*. Rust-red chalybeate (iron) spring water flows through the well, and is said to have healing powers. Lower down in the gardens, the water emerges from a spout and can be sampled by visitors. The shaft of the well is alleged to have been constructed by the Druids.

According to tradition, the Essene, Joseph of Arimathea, settled near Chalice Well having brought the chalice of the Lord's supper to Glastonbury in AD 37: The thorn tree above the lion's head in Chalice Well gardens reminds us of how Joseph is said to have placed his staff into the ground on Wearyall hill and in that spot grew and flowered a hawthorn tree.

In 1958, Wellesley Tudor Pole, founded the Chalice Well Trust, with the object of preserving the well and surrounding land so that it would continue as a sacred shrine. The prime purpose is for it to be kept as a peaceful sanctuary.

67. Chalice Well

68. Chalice Well gardens

Glastonbury is on the A39 south of Bristol and 24 kilometres from junction 23 of the M5, east of Bridgwater.

Food and Drink: In Glastonbury at No. 3, Magdalene Street (0458 32129); or George & Pilgrims, High Street (0458 31146).

GLASTONBURY

Power point – abbey – tor – legend – zodiac

Somerset   MAP REF. ST4938

Today the town of Glastonbury plays host to the mysteries both ancient and modern. The surrounding countryside is imprinted with powerful legends and places of worship, while the town itself has spawned a host of 'New Age' venues, from shops selling crystals for healing to every kind of complementary therapy. A walk down the main street will tempt the visitor into the Gothic Image bookshop – probably the best source of material on the mystical history of Glastonbury and its environs. There is also the Glastonbury Experience, a complex of 'esoteric' shops, and the mystical crystal world of Shambhalla.

In the bustle of this busy town it is easy to loose sight of the atmosphere that we, as pilgrims to the sacred and ancient, are seeking. Glastonbury Tor is the most prominent and easily identifiable such location. The remainder of St Michael's church at the top of the tor is a reminder that sometimes England suffers from earthquakes, as the shell is said to have remained in its present form since being destroyed by a quake in the thirteenth century. However, the tower is certainly later than the thirteenth century, but there has been a

69. Glastonbury Tor

70. *Glastonbury Abbey*

Christian settlement on or near the tor since at least the fourth century.

The connection between Glastonbury and the legends of the Holy Grail, and with Joseph of Arimathea (see also the separate entry under 'Chalice Well', the gardens and healing well being located just a short distance from the town centre) have been well promoted by the romantic literature developed in the thirteenth and fourteenth centuries.

When the ecclesiastical historians came to write the story of the origins of the Christian church in Britain, they knew little and had to fall back on the support of legend. The honour of our first evangelist was bestowed on Joseph of Arimathea. Joseph, they said, arrived from Jerusalem with 150 disciples early in the first century AD to found an oratory at Glastonbury, bringing with him the sacred thorn tree and two silver cruets, one containing the blood, the other the sweat, of the crucified Christ.

It was generally conceded, however, that Joseph and his 150 disciples could not have crossed the straights of Dover on the shirt of Josephes, the saint's son, as John of Glastonbury tells us (c. 1400); and that the monastery at Glastonbury was founded not by Joseph in the first century, but by Celtic monks some time late in the fifth.

Referring now to the remains of the Abbey, careful exploration will reveal much occult symbolism, such as the mediaeval fish inscribed in the fabric of the western side of the high wall of the Abbey. The holy thorn in the Abbey grounds, to the left of the main public entrance, which flowers in mid-winter, is said to be a cutting from Joseph's original thorn. The centre of the excavated grounds of the mined Abbey is marked with a plaque where the supposed remains of Arthur and Guinevere were discovered in 1191, seven years after the abbey was burnt down.

Marked out across the Somerset landscape, within a circle ten miles across, lies the Glastonbury Zodiac, rediscovered in 1929 by Katherine Maltwood. At the top of the wheel beside Glastonbury town and encompassing the Tor, lies the ancient Air sign of Aquarius.

Glastonbury is at the junction of the A361 and A39, south-west of Bath. The Tor is clearly visible from all approach roads.

Food and Drink: In Glastonbury at the George & Pilgrim, High Street (0458 31146); or at No. 3, Magdalene Street (0458 32129).

EAST QUANTOXHEAD

Church – alchemy – symbols

Somerset   MAP REF. ST1343

The carved series of 'Seals of Solomon', found on a bench end in the parish church, depict in occult symbolism the four elements of Earth, Air, Fire and Water. Today, these four elements have become interpreted as four aspects of the human personality, linked with sensations, thoughts, imagination or intuition, and emotions, respectively. Within the symbolism in this parish church can be found a numerological sequence of one central boss, two triangles, three points to each triangle, four petals to each flower, five for the quintessence, six points to the interlaced triangles, etc., through to twelve. The seal of Solomon was often worn as a talisman, an essential one to have when evoking spirits and very efficacious for securing all that the wearer desires, so much so that the most evil genii cannot injure the person wearing it.

East Quantoxhead is west of Bridgwater, north of the A39.

Food and Drink: In Watchet at Downfield, 16 St Decuman's Road (0984 31267).

THE GREEN MAN, BISHOP'S LYDEARD

Symbols – nature spirits

Somerset   MAP REF. ST1629

Carved in wood relief in the parish church there is a late fifteenth-century Green Man, an image of pagan nature spirits, symbol of death and renewal. It is interesting to locate such pagan images within the precincts of a Christian church. Why do they sometimes survive, despite the paranoia which often exists to interpret them as evil. The old ways of nature religion die hard. Perhaps they remain because they are becoming relevant to today's search for meaning and a new reverence for nature and the environment.

Bishop's Lydeard is on the A358, north-west of Taunton.

Food and Drink: In Taunton at the Corner House, Park Street (0823 284683); or St Quintin, Bridgwater Road (0823 259171).

ST BRANNOCK'S CHURCH, BRAUNTON

Church – alchemy – hermeticism

Devon   MAP REF. SS4836

Carvings of occult symbols can be found in this church.

Noteably those of alchemical origin are a man being swallowed by a dragon, a pelican feeding her young with her own blood, and a triple face with only four eyes. In alchemy, the dragon is a symbol of destructive forces, the beginning part of the process; the pelican is a common image for Christ – we are the young, our blood is His blood, our life is His; the numbers three and four have their significance too, three standing for the trinity, four for the earth. The imagery is ancient in ancestry and far from that associated with Christian symbolism.

Braunton is on the A361, north-west of Barnstaple.

Food and Drink: In Braunton at Poyers Hotel and Restaurant, Wrafton (0271 812149); or Otters, 30 Caen Street (0271 813633).

HIGHER GUNSTONE LANE, BIDEFORD

Witchcraft – magic

Devon MAP REF. SS4526

In 1682, in Higher Gunstone Lane, Temperance Lloyd, a self-confessed witch met the Devil in the form of a huge black man. Susanna Edwards belonged to the same witches' coven as Temperance. She also claimed to have met the Devil and the two of them were hanged for practising witchcraft. It was common in the witch hunts of the seventeenth century for women to believe that they were witches, perhaps simply through particular dreams or imaginative experiences. Forms of mystical experience were taboo as the church held this power to itself. This meant that any form of vision – particularly if experienced by a woman – came from the Devil.

Higher Gunstone Lane runs up the hill to the west of Bideford.

Food and Drink: In Barnstaple at the Royal & Fortesque, Boutport Street (0271 42289); or Lynwood House, Bishops Tawton (0271 43695).

EGLOSKERRY

Church – alchemy – symbolism

Cornwall   MAP REF. SX2786

All four archangels, Michael, Gabriel, Raphael and Uriel, are depicted on the stained glass, made in 1905, in the village church. In esoteric lore, the archangels are each part of a four-fold system of correspondence, a *quaternio*. For example, Gabriel is the archangel of winter, Raphael, the healer, of spring, Uriel of summer, charged with the continuance and health of the earth, and, finally, Michael, bearer of the sword of Light, rules the autumn. Gabriel rules the astrological element of Water, Raphael rules Air, Uriel rules Earth, and Michael rules Fire.

There is a blocked-up door in the church's north wall and an early Saxon dragon indicates that this is an example of a 'Devil's Door'. Esoteric symbols from many periods can be found within this church.

Take the B3524 west of Launceston, then Egloskerry is on a minor road west of Langore and St Stephens.

Food and Drink: In Launceston at the White Hart, Broad Street (0566 2013).

ST CLETHER

Church – holy well

Cornwall   MAP REF. SX2084

The chapel at St Clether, dedicated to St Clederus, has been constructed to allow the water overflow from the village's holy well to pass through the end of the chapel, beneath the altar, where the body of the saint was originally laid. The pagan, magical waters were thus rendered holy by their contact with the saint's aura.

St Clether is signposted south of the A395. The well is to the west of the church, across hilly grasslands.

Food and Drink: In Launceston at the White Hart, Broad Street (0566 2013).

194

TINTAGEL

Legends

Cornwall   MAP REF. SX0588

Tintagel head, to the west of the village is the pre-
carious site for the castle of King Arthur, the famous
mythological Camelot. Whoever inhabited this castle
must have had a good head for heights. It was built in
1145, so the existing stonework cannot represent the
actual domain of the sixth-century king. The nearby
Merlin's Cave is on the shingle beach below and there
are indications of sixth- and seventh-century Celtic
Christian settlements in the area.

Tintagel is on the B3263, south of Boscastle.

Food and Drink: In Tintagel at the Atlantic View,
Treknow (0840 770221); or Bossiney House (0840
770240).

DYMOND MONUMENT, CAMELFORD

Power point – monument – haunting

Cornwall   MAP REF. SX1083

Charlotte Dymond, a servant girl said to be murdered
by a jealous lover, Matthew Weeks, in 1844, is among

the many ghosts that haunt Bodmin Moor. She is now believed to have committed suicide and Weeks hanged for the crime as the result of a conspiracy. The monument was raised by locals in commemoration of this event. Above the monument stands Rough Tor, once the sight of a chapel dedicated to St Michael.

The monument is on the moorland side of the Helland bridge, below Rough Tor, signposted from the B3266 south of Camelford.

Food and Drink: In Bodmin at Hotel Allegro, Higher Bore Street (0208 3480); or Westberry, Rhind Street (0208 2772).

JAMAICA INN

Haunting

Cornwall   MAP REF. SX1777

This is a place to exercise one's psychic powers. Can you feel anything in the atmosphere here, or tell what really happened? Jamaica Inn is the site of a haunting by a sailor and smuggler who was murdered there in the eighteenth century. Daphne du Maurier popularised the inn in her novel of the same name.

It can be found north of the A30, south of Bolventor.

Food and Drink: In Bodmin at Hotel Allegro, 50 Higher Bore Street (0208 3480); or Westberry, Rhind Street (0208 2772).

TEMPLARS CHAPEL, BODMIN MOOR

Rituals – legend

Cornwall   MAP REF. SX1975

The Knight's Templars had a chapel in the place still called Temple. King Arthur figures large in this area. Near Camelford is the supposed site of Arthur's last battle, the site of his legendary palace, and Dozmary Pool, the lake into which Excalibur was thrown, after his death.

Bodmin Moor is traversed by the A30, between Launceston and Bodmin.

Food and Drink: In Bodmin at Hotel Allegro, 50 Higher Bore Street (0208 3480); or Westberry, Rhind Street (0208 2772).

WARLEGGAN

Haunting – church

Cornwall   MAP REF. SX1569

Ralph Tramur, the son of the second rector of the church of St Bartholomew was generally regarded as a heretic and witch, while the curate of 1774, Francis Cole, is said still to haunt the road outside Trengoffe, where the wheels of his carriage are heard at night. The church is in the 'loneliest village on Bodmin

Moor', and sports animal images on the Norman capitals inside the church, where there are signs of a 'Devil's Door' in the northern fabric.

Approached via the minor road between Cardinham and St Neot, Warleggan lies between the A30(T) and the A38(T), east of Bodmin.

Food and Drink: In Bodmin at Hotel Allegro, Higher Bore Street (0208 3480); or Westberry, Rhind Street (0208 2772).

THE CHEESEWRING

Natural formation – legend

Cornwall   MAP REF. SX2672

To achieve a quality of the mystical and to evoke the imagination, an occult site does not need to be man-made. Sometimes, sites possess the quality of appearing man-made when in fact it is nature that has shaped the landscape into evocative forms. Supposedly a natural formation, this weird pile of rocks on Bodmin Moor was believed to be the dwelling place of a druid who possessed a cup of gold. The cup, whose contents were inexhaustible, was always offered to thirsty travellers. One tried to drink the cup dry, but failed. In a rage he rode off with the cup, whereupon his horse fell over the rocks and he was killed. The cup was buried with him. This is not all. In 1818, a nearby cairn called King Arthur's Grave was opened and a gold cup, dated around 1500 BC was found.

71. The Hill with the Cheesewring, Bodmin Moor

The Cheesewring is west of the B3254, travelling north from Liskeard.

Food and Drink: In Liskeard at the Lord Eliot, Castle Street (0579 42717); or Webbs, The Parade (0579 43675).

ST NUN'S WELL, PELYNT

Holy well – legend

Cornwall MAP REF. SX2356

Known locally as St Ninnie's Well and Piskies' Well, pins are thrown into it to keep the little people happy, and to obtain their cooperation in successful farming. The granite basin into which the water flowed can be seen inside the well's doorway, and is decorated with circles and crosses. One farmer wanted to use the basin as a pig trough, so he fastened his oxen to the basin to drag it clear. All appeared to be going well for a while until the chain which held it snapped. The basin rolled back again to the well, made a sharp turn and leapt into its old position, where it has remained ever since.

The village is on the B3359 which runs north from the A387, west of Looe.

Food and Drink: In Pelynt at Jubilee Inn (0503 20312).

ST GURON'S WELL, BODMIN

Holy well

Cornwall   MAP REF. SX0767

Because water is one of the basic compounds necessary for life, it has always been attributed with magical powers – and what could be more magical than the ability to sustain life. The waters of St Guron's well, to the west of St Petroc's church, were known for their healing power, specifically for eye troubles. It is likely that the well was in use for some centuries before the introduction of Christianity to the area. This is a good example of the practice of early Christians not to obliterate the old sacred sites, nor to set up new ones of their own, but simply to adapt the old for their own purposes. This was one secret of their success.

St Guron's Well can be found north of the A30, to the north-east of Bodmin.

200

Food and Drink: In Bodmin at Hotel Allegro, 50 Higher Bore Street (0208 3480); or Westberry, Rhind Street (0208 2772).

PENHALE SANDS

Standing stone – legend – power point

Cornwall   MAP REF. SW7756

There are many standing stones in this county, called 'crosses'. St Piran's Cross stands on a long stretch of sandhills, under which is said to be buried the large city of Langarrow. Over 1000 years ago, because of the wickedness of the inhabitants, a violent storm arose which lasted for three days and nights, causing the entire city and its population to be buried beneath the sand. Legend or not, in 1835 the shifting sands revealed a buried church. The age of St Piran's Cross is uncertain, but it is thought to be pre-Christian. The shape, with a round head and two side projections above a tapering base, echoes the shape of the Egyptian ankh, symbol of life. Many such crosses are really ancient sacred stones that have been Christianised, sometimes simply by the addition of a cross in later ages.

The Sands run north from Perranporth to Penhale Point, west of the A3075 from Newquay to Redruth.

Food and Drink: In Perranporth at Promenade (0872 573118); or Beach Dunes, Ramoth Way, Reen Sands (0872 572263).

TRENCROM HILL

Earthwork – legend

Cornwall   MAP REF. SW5236

The summit of Trencrom Hill, near Lelant, was at one time occupied. Traces of hut circles have been found there and also a massive rampart which used the rock formations. Legend describes how the inhabitants, ill-tempered giants, hid their treasure in the hill where it is now guarded by spriggans – the ghosts of giants, found only among the ancient stones up on the moorlands. About 200 years ago, a tin miner actually managed to grab a handful of the gold and escape – no mean feat.

The hill lies south of Carbis Bay and west of Lelant, approached by minor roads.

Food and Drink: In Carbis Bay at Cornwallis, Headland Road (0736 795294); or St Uny (0736 795011).

ST SENARA, ZENNOR

Church – legends

Cornwall   MAP REF. SW4538

In the parish church is the figure of a mermaid, probably the most famous in Cornwall. It is carved on a plank which was once part of a mediaeval bench-end. It is told how a woman in a long dress used to attend services to listen to the singing of the chorister Matthew Trewhella. One Sunday she lured him down to the village stream, and then down to Pendour Cove, where Matthew disappeared, to become the husband of the mermaid.

The cross on the top of the south porch of the church is said to have great healing powers.

Zennor is north of the B3306, west of St Ives.

Food and Drink: In St Ives at Boskerris, Boskerris Road, Carbis Bay (0736 795295); or Chy-an-Dour, Trelyon Avenue (0736 796436).

LANYON QUOIT, PENZANCE

Standing stone – earthwork

Cornwall   MAP REF. SW4334

Lanyon Quoit, consisting of three main uprights,

72. *Lanyon Quoit*

holding a huge flat slab above them, was re-erected in about 1815–16, after falling during a storm. Records show that it was originally high enough for a person on horseback to pass underneath. Traces of the earth mound which covered the stones can just be seen close by.

Travelling from Penzance to St Just on the A3071, turn off to the right at Newbridge, in the direction of Morvah.

Food and Drink: In Newbridge at Enzo of Newbridge (0736 63777).

MEN-AN-TOL

Holed stone – legend – rituals

Cornwall   MAP REF. SW4035

There is a significant connection between the word 'holy' and the word 'heal', which implies making 'whole' again. Religious experiences are often associated with miraculous healings, and it is therefore no surprise when the legends which attach to the site of the old religion are to do with healing. The large, holed stone near Morvah is also known as the Crick Stone. There are other holed stones in Cornwall, and indeed in other parts of the world. They are often associated with the cure of certain illnesses and children were once passed through Men-an-Tol when they were suffering from rickets. This was achieved by either crawling or being lifted through the hole. This particular stone was also consulted by people who wished to know about their future love life. There are

73. Men-An-Tol

four stones at this site, said to be over 4000 years old. The astronomer, Norman Lockyer, has suggested they has astronomical significance, sighting other distant stones to form links between these and important star positions.

This particular stone was also an oracle – two pins put crosswise on top of the stone acquired a 'peculiar motion'. This was interpreted in answer to a question put to the stone.

Morvah is on the B3306 road between St Just and St Ives.

Food and Drink: In St Ives at Boskerris, Boskerris Road (0736 795295); or Ocean Breezes, West Place, Barnoon – close to the old town (0736 795587).

THE NINE MAIDENS, BOSKEDNAN

Stone circle

Cornwall   MAP REF. SW4535

The name given to this small circle is echoed elsewhere in the county, and is a reference to a legend that the nine maidens were turned to stone for dancing on a Sunday. This small circle lies off the beaten track in an area of lonely moorland, untouched by civilisation. Perhaps the musicians were the Pipers, who are now two standing stones near Lamorna, not far away.

Take the road from Penzance to Zennor and turn left through New Mill.

Food and Drink: In Penzance at Sea and Horses, 6 Alexandra Terrace (0736 61961); or Estoril, Morrab Road (0736 62468).

74. Nine Maidens circle

75. *Blind Fiddler*

THE BLIND FIDDLER

Standing stone – legends

Cornwall MAP REF. SW4228

Cornwall is a happy hunting ground for travellers interested in the lore surrounding mystical ancient standing stones. One reason why legends and myths grow attached to megalithic monuments is that no one can prove definitely what their original purpose and use was. Modern earth mysteries research is shedding new light on dry archaeological data. The standing stone at this particular map reference is one of several single standing stones given the names of musicians. This particular 'Blind Fiddler' was turned to stone for making music on the Sabbath. Whatever the reason, the result is an impressive 3.3 metres of solid stone.

The stone can be found near Catchall, off the A30 Penzance to Land's End road.

Food and Drink: In Penzance at the Sea and Horses, 6 Alexandra Terrace (0736 61961); or Southern Comfort, Alexandra Terrace (0736 66333). Both are on the sea front.

ST MICHAEL'S MOUNT

Power point – leys – legend

Cornwall MAP REF. SW5130

This site is attributed with being the most holy place in Cornwall, as well as a crossing point for ley lines, and thus a major occult power point. It has in modern times become a place of pilgrimage and is said to take its name from a hermit who had a vision of the Archangel Michael while living on the mount. St Michael is the archangel associated in particular with the Age of Aquarius and therefore sites dedicated to him have particular significance for the New Age pilgrim. St Michael's Mount is supposed to have been built by giants, in particular the ancient giant, Cormoran.

The Mount is connected with the mainland by a causeway some forty metres in width formed by fragments of rock and pebbles compacted by two currents of the sea sweeping round the rock at the flooding of the tide. This causeway is covered at high water when the Mount becomes an islet.

The Mount was known in the Cornish language as *Cara Cowz in Clouze*, or 'The Grey Rock in the Woods', a curious name which can be explained by the vestiges of a submerged forest extending for some miles around the base of the rock.

The Mount is off Marazion, signposted from the A394, east of Penzance.

Food and Drink: In Penzance at Sea and Horses, 6 Alexandra Terrace (0736 61961); or Southern Comfort, Alexandra Terrace (0736 66333).

DOWSING AT ANCIENT SITES

The following description of dowsing or 'divining' techniques is extracted from Dowsing For Health *by Arthur Bailey, Past President of and Scientific Adviser to The British Society of Dowsers.*

*The use of dowsing at ancient sacred sites is being used increasingly as an effective tool for delving into the minds of the original builders, investigating local earth energies and ley lines, and for investigating underground properties, such as mineral deposits, water flows, and geological faults. Try it and see if it works for you. (*Dowsing For Health *is a Quantum book, published by W. Foulsham & Co.)*

TOOLS OF THE TRADE

Over the years there have been many dowsing tools developed. Many of these have had temporary acceptance, and then fallen into disuse. The first thing that should be born in mind is that there is much folklore, still, about dowsing tools. I well remember one lady who looked admiringly at a beechwood pendulum that I was using. 'That's a lovely pendulum,' she said, 'It's so important to use natural materials for accurate results. What sort of thread are you using? It looks like silk.' 'Well actually', I replied, 'it's made of Nylon.' After that I felt that I had been consigned to the ranks of the inaccurate dowsers.

The dowsing reaction is on the body of the dowser, not on the rod or pendulum being used. Another important point is that it is far better to feel at home with the tools that you use, and it is irrelevant what you actually use for your dowsing. What matters is, does it work for you? I have a treasured memory from a Congress of the British Society of Dowsers at Harrowgate. There had been an afternoon of dowsing at Fountains Abbey, and a group of us had gone into a tea-shop in Ripon for afternoon tea. One of the group decided to dowse over the scones to see if they would disagree with her. She opened her handbag and produced from it a toy mouse. She then held it up by its tail and used it as a pendulum. It demonstrated that one really can use anything, but this incident would hardly instil confidence into a sceptical onlooker!

Consider the forked stick first, as it seems to have been the first recorded dowsing tool. The stick need not be wood; plastic or thin metal bent to the correct shape will do just as well. If you try with wood, it is important to select a nice 'vee' branch of supple wood. Hazel is the classical wood, but rhododendron, dogwood, and other strong flexible woods are good. If in doubt, try it and see but note that brittle or too flexible woods will either break or collapse in your hands. It is important how the stick is held. The palms are upwards and the stick is spring-loaded by the outer parts of the fork being bent open from their natural position. When holding a forked rod this way, which may feel unnatural to the beginner, any rotation of the forearms will make the rod move. If the tops of the forearms rotate towards each other, the tip of the rod will dip. Conversely, if the tops of the arms move away from each other, the rod tip will rise. Angling the wrists to increase or decrease the spring-loading of the rod will increase or decrease the sensitivity of the rod. Too much tension in the rod will either make it unstable so it jumps up or down on its own, or it will break. Hence the importance of a suitable material for the rod.

Having mastered holding a forked rod, the next thing is to try it out. Really the best place for this is out in the open country away from prying eyes. Most people experience quite a strong reaction from underground water flows, and there is something natural and fundamental about using a forked rod to look for water in the countryside. What one is looking for is a reaction from the rod, either up or down. Never mind which way it moves, or wondering whether it is going in the right direction: there is no right direction. What matters is that it moves in a repeatable manner. If it moves every time at a certain place, and you don't know what is there, never mind; we will be looking later at methods of analysis. At this stage it is a matter of experiencing movements and increasing confidence.

But suppose that there is no suitable material for a forked rod where you live. What then? You can make a suitable rod from two long bits of plastic bound together at one end – long thin plastic knitting needles have been used by some people. Whalebone from Victorian corsets was once popular, but thankfully whalebone is no longer available. Basically, two pieces of anything springy that can be bound together at one end are suitable for use. However, it can be quite difficult to hold such rods correctly.

Suppose that you find the forked rod too difficult to use, or perhaps you get no response at all, what then? Perhaps the next dowsing instrument to try is the angle-rod. Although the pendulum is more widely used for healing applications, it is much more susceptible to autosuggestion. Angle-rods have a nice solid feel to them, and can be used for healing work if the pendulum does not work for you, even though the pendulum is easier to use. Also there is something to be said for locating such physical things as water and pipes before venturing into the rather more difficult areas.

Angle-rods are very simple to make, and need consist of nothing more than two bent pieces of wire. The diameter and length of the wire is not too critical. Large sparkler wires left after bonfire night will even do at a pinch. It is best to use fairly thick wire so that the rods are not seriously affected by light winds. A diameter of about 2 mm will do well, and before bending, the wire lengths should be about 30 cm. Each wire should then be bent at right angles about 9 cm from one end. Also the wire is best made from heavy metal such as steel to prevent it being too sensitive to the wind. The wire in steel (not aluminium) coat-hangers is fine when straightened out. The rods are then held, one in each hand, with the longer length of the 'L' pointing forward. The rods must only be held lightly so that they are free to swing. If this is found to be too difficult, then hollow handles can be used. Bamboo may be used, but I find that it is neater to use old cheap ballpoint pens. The Bic ones are ideal. If the innards of such pens are pulled out with a pair of pliers, then hollow handles with a bottom plastic bung are formed. Again the shorter length of the 'L' needs to be just a little bit longer than the holder so that the rods do not foul the tops of the tubes. The rods can be dropped into these holders and the pens then held instead of the rods.

I use angle-rods that I made myself with ball-races in the handles. This enables me to use thick brass horizontal rods of about 3 mm diameter. These are easy to hold, and operate well in all but strong winds. Apart from that, they also look more professional than bent welding wires, even though the latter will work just as well on a calm day.

Learning to walk with angle-rods can be quite difficult. The art is to walk slowly without jolting the rods, keeping the front of the rods dropped down slightly. If the rod tips are above the horizontal, then inevitably the rods will swing round back towards you. Indeed the best way of controlling the sensitivity is by adjusting how far the tips of the rods are below the horizontal.

If the rods are initially parallel, then for most people when walking over an underground feature, the tips of the rods will move towards each other. For a few people the rods move apart, so if the rods move apart for you, then there is nothing to worry about. Please don't think that your 'polarity' is reversed or that you are suffering from incorrect diet or ley lines! It is simply that people react differently, nothing more.

What drives the angle-rods is exactly the same as for the forked rod – a slight unconscious rotation of the forearms. If the tops of the forearms rotate towards each other, then the rods will move towards each other; a movement away will cause the rods to move out. It is the change in balance between the flexor and extensor muscles that makes the rods move. If your rods move outwards, it means that the change in muscular balance just happens to have a net result that is the opposite direction to the majority of people, nothing else.

Most people experience a reaction with angle-rods, unless they are totally convinced that it will not work. Often the reaction is initially small and may be hard to see. However, perseverance pays off. Initially my angle-rod reactions were small and only just noticeable. Within a year they were strong, but it needed practice to gain the confidence that was necessary to give such positive results. I was sceptical when I first tried dowsing and there is no doubt that it adversely affected my dowsing sensitivity at the beginning.

Like the forked rod, it is useful, though by no means essential, to try angle-rods out in the countryside. Angle-rods have rather more versatility than the forked rod, which soon becomes evident with use. Suppose that you are looking for water, and unknown to you there is an underground aquifer (this is the academically correct name for an underground stream) running parallel to the direction that you are walking. Under these conditions the rods will often both move and point to the side of you where the water is flowing, thus showing that the nearest water is to one side of you, rather than in front. This can save a lot of leg-work at times.

THE PENDULUM

There are other forms of rods, but they are of little importance except for some specialised uses where they may be helpful. The pendulum can be made of any material; what matters is that its operator feels at home with it. A fairly heavy finger ring on a piece of cotton thread will work well for many people. Some dowsers use metal pendulums on metal chains, others crystal pendulums on fine silver or gold chains, others use wooden or plastic pendulums. The main point is that the pendulum bob needs to be sufficiently heavy so that its movements can be felt by the fingers.

Again, it is an unconscious movement of the hand that makes the instrument move. In this case the pendulum is given small imperceptible pushes from the hand at the same rate as the natural frequency of oscillation of the pendulum. For this reason, many people find that there is a certain length of string to the pendulum that gives the best response. A satisfactory way of determining the optimum length is to start by using a short thread of between 5 to 8 centimetres in length. The pendulum can than be successively lengthened until the most sensitive results are obtained.

One way of getting used to the pendulum is to 'tell' it to go in, say, a clockwise direction. The pendulum may then begin to rotate in that direction without any conscious physical intervention. For more speedy results the pendulum can initially be swung in a straight line before telling it what to do. This action of the mind in being able to unconsciously alter the swing of a pendulum has been known for a long time, and it is often used to argue that dowsing is therefore wishful thinking. This effect must always be borne in mind, as it shows just how easy it is for wishful thinking to influence one's dowsing. This effect can occur whatever dowsing implement is used, but it tends to be more noticeable with a pendulum.

Checking for underground water flows with a pendulum can be done, but it is not as easy as with angle-rods or a forked rod. It is a matter of walking slowly along and watching for the pendulum to either start moving or change its mode of movement. For instance, it may change from a straight-line swing to moving with a circular swing. The main difficulty is that the action of walking tends to move the pendulum, so one has to walk very steadily and carefully for the results to be unambiguous.

The pendulum is more useful for indoor use, and as it only needs one hand it is easy to use. Also, it is capable of even more responses than the angle-rods, as we shall see. This makes it useful for healing applications as it can give more graded answers than 'yes' or 'no'.

CODING METHODS

What sort of reaction should the pendulum give? One simple way is to just hold the pendulum and ask it the question, 'Show me which movement indicates a positive answer.' For many people this proves to be a clockwise circle when viewed from above. This is the method that I always recommend. It may take time for the pendulum to move, and if so give it a small backward and forward swing and watch to see if it changes into a circle. Above all, don't be disheartened if nothing much happens at first. For some people it takes a bit of practice before the pendulum moves at all reliably. After all, you are trying to forge a neuro-muscular link with the intuitive part of the brain, so don't get impatient if nothing much happens at first, and don't become tense trying, nothing inhibits dowsing more than tension. A small amount of alcohol can help one to relax, but try to avoid becoming like one dowser who could only dowse accurately when he was very drunk.

Suppose that you now obtain a definite pendulum movement which indicates a positive dowsing answer. This is equivalent to the angle-rods crossing or the forked stick lifting. The pendulum, however, has many movements available. It can swing in straight lines at varying angles, it can make ellipses at varying angles both clockwise and anticlockwise, also clockwise and anticlockwise circles. In other words there is the capability for it to indicate more than just a 'yes' response, and this is the key to its use in healing applications.

Holding the pendulum by its string, ask it to indicate what movement indicates negative or 'no'. For many people this is an anticlockwise circle, but again don't be surprised if you find something different. If you now obtain two clearly different movements, then you can check food without a rule, but with no real idea of how good or bad it is for you. Hold the pendulum over foods with the mental question, 'Is this food good for me to eat?'

You can get surprises with either 'yes' or 'no' answers. I once demonstrated dowsing at a theatre bar to some friends. I dowsed over a pint of beer and, much to my surprise, I found a clear 'yes' answer. This was not what I had been expecting at all, and caused a lot of amusement as I had been telling them how beer was bad for me and that it would show up as bad with my dowsing. The result could have been due to the vitamin B content of the beer, as I could well have been suffering from a vitamin B deficiency that day. This shows again how careful one has to be to avoid generalisations.

There was one very positive thing that came out of that particular demonstration. If your dowsing can give you surprises like that – giving results that are totally unexpected – then it shows that autosuggestion is not overriding the dowsing faculty. It indicates that your dowsing is getting to the point, even if not completely there, where it can always be relied on.

LEY LINES

There is much confusion and dissention in this area, and there seem to be as many ideas as there are enthusiasts pursuing the subject. The original concept of leys came from Alfred Watkins. He noticed that there appeared to be long straight tracks connecting places of antiquity such as churches, dolmens and barrows. On the Ordnance Survey map, as many as five ancient sites could be found lying along the same straight line or track, within a significantly short distance and accurate to within one hundred feet or so. Watkins surmised that these alignments were deliberate and called them 'ley lines'. It was later that Guy Underwood did some dowsing work and came up with the idea that there were also natural energy lines ('track lines', 'water lines' and 'aquastats') which he called 'geodetic lines'. Some of these were found along the straight (or ley) lines that linked ancient sites and the geodetic lines could be detected by the use of dowsing. Underwood also did much dowsing around the sites of antiquity themselves.

That was what started it all off. After about ten years 'ley hunting' got under way. The renewed modern interest in ancient sites catalysed the whole thing and many eager-beavers started dowsing for ley lines, sometimes I suspect with little idea what they were dowsing for. It was also of note that not everyone came up with the same energy patterns as Guy Underwood had done, indeed the majority of people achieved quite different results. This difference between the results of 'energy fields' dowsed by different people is a factor that turns up time and time again. I would like to repeat my warnings of not being carried away by wishful thinking. It is all too easy, in such a nebulous area, to dowse and find the products of expectation or imagination, rather than what is really there. Also when dowsing for something that is, after all, pretty intangible, it is easy to phrase one's dowsing question incorrectly or for it to be too broad in concept.

So just what are these ley lines? My own dowsing

would suggest that there are several different categories of them, although their effects may be similar.

Firstly, there seem to be straight energy lines that one can detect by dowsing, these lines affecting the health of people adversely. These lines do not appear to be linked with obvious alignments through churches and ancient monuments. In the absence of any other information, it can be assumed that these are natural energy forces associated with the earth.

Next, there are straight energy lines that *do* align with churches, ancient monuments, etc. Usually these do not affect people adversely – in fact to the contrary, they can have healing effects. One should beware however, it is not necessarily wise to live on such a line, one can have too much of a good thing. These lines are probably natural, ancient people having deliberately sited their places of worship on them, their preference being for a point where two or more such lines crossed.

Finally, there are those lines that are man-made. Sometimes these appear spontaneously where there is serious illness at a site which was previously clear. Sometimes these lines are made by acts of ritual or other mind-concentrating methods. In other words, it appears that energy lines can be created (or rather activated) by conscious or unconscious action.

One can attempt to classify lines, dowsing then being used to categorise the types of line, but this will not be conclusive. One may be simply dowsing for what one's conscious mind believes. Ultimately, all one can do is steadily and carefully gather factual information and look for patterns in that information.

Be that as it may, it remains a fact that many people have taken to ley hunting both by looking for alignments on maps and also by dowsing for ley lines. To many people it has become a fascinating and valuable interest, and their researches will bare fruit for future generations.

INDEX BY NAME